BRYNCA'S LOW

A Revised and Updated History
Of the Village of Brinklow,
Warwickshire

DIANE LINDSAY

BRYNCA'S LOW

A Revised & Updated History of the Village of Brinklow

Book produced by Tony Rattigan

First published 1995 by Brynca's Low Books
Updated 2017

CONTENTS

INTRODUCTION TO THE 2ND EDITION

This book owes everything to Brinklow History Group, sadly now defunct, which was formed in 1992 by a very small group of enthusiasts with a passion for our historic village. Thankfully we collected an extraordinary amount of information, photos, stories and details of past times, from people who are sadly no longer here to tell us what they knew.

With what we gathered, we put on a modest Nostalgia Exhibition, which was so popular I began to research properly and wrote the first Brynca's Low. Much of that still stands in this book but over the years not only has that print run sold out, so much more has been discovered it needs to be shared with those of you who love Brinklow, who have ancestral roots here or just love history as it happened to real people rather than Kings, Queens and Barons.

Over the years I have kept the faith, continued researching, stored the Great Brinklow Exhibition on top of the wardrobe in my spare room, and trotted bits of it out whenever an occasion presented itself. It's now time to get all those new bits of paper out and rewrite the book for another Exhibition, this time for Brinklow's second Scarecrow Festival. Last year's was wonderful, a fantastic example of community spirit.

This year's Festival will be superb, bigger than ever and more than deserves a new revised history to mark it.

My main focus of research in this new updated edition has been into Brinklow names; place, field and personal names connected with the village and recorded since medieval times. Not only has it been a fascinating study of the cheerfully nonchalant attitude to handwriting, spelling and grammar by our forebears, for me it has done something far more significant. Because names are so tied to the environment, studying them has enabled me to step back imaginatively into the past and discover the lifestyles, the important issues, the attitudes, even the diets of Brinklow people since there was indeed a functioning castle on the hill and a forest as far as the eye could see outside the village. We in Brinklow walk alongside the past every day.

I hope this second edition will be enjoyed by everyone, not only local people, because the history of our village is really the history of England. With new, more and better pictures, some new chapters and appendices for those that want to study who lived here when, where they acted out their daily lives, and why they did what they did, I hope you find it interesting enough to take up local and family history as the glorious pastimes they are and add your own discoveries to the sum of our understanding of the past.

Diane Lindsay
Brinklow May 2017

Part of the parish of Brinklow, showing the castle mound and the main street. (From the Parish Glebe Map 1838. Original in Warwick Record Office.)

Brynca's Low

Brinklow Tump with elms circa 1950

Brinklow's most notable topographical feature is the imposing grassy mound behind the church, known locally as "The Tump", or "The Big Hill". Built on a natural rise, and offering a commanding and striking view of the surrounding countryside, the hill and its earthworks represent one of the best-preserved Norman motte and bailey castle sites in the country. However, the name of Brinklow itself suggests a much older settled community, or at least that it was a site of some importance to people long before the Norman Conquest.

The name is thought to originate from two Old English elements: the personal name *Brynca*, and the word *hlaw* meaning "hill" in the sense of tumulus or burial mound. This ancient derivation implies that there was almost certainly a man-made "tump" here long before the Normans exploited the site to build their castle, clearly drawn to it by the strategic nature of the hill as a defensive sighting point, and its position on the Roman Fosse Way.

There is some dispute as to the exact location of the Fosse Way as it passes through Brinklow. Some authorities suggest that the original route would have passed behind the Tump, from Bretford, joining up again at Stretton-under-Fosse, and certainly, from today's map, this seems the logical straight route. Ell Lane has also been suggested as a possible echo of the ancient road, gaining its unusual name as a corruption of "Hill" Lane. However, there are arguments in favour of the theory that the present road and the old Roman military road are one and the same. The Roman engineers, where possible, did not build their roads uphill, preferring to go round them; the present route is the least hilly. Not all Roman roads were totally straight -where a natural obstacle occurred, their roads kink to avoid it. It is also known that they preferred to leave native sacred sites intact, rather than disturb them. Brinklow Hill may well have had some significance to the ancient Coritani people, whose capital was Leicester, but who may have strayed in isolated small settlements southwards; the exact boundaries of their lands are not known.

Brinklow Hill was the subject of much debate in the *"Transactions, Excursions and Reports"* of the Archaeological Section of the Birmingham and Midland Institute, published in 1873. It was noted that it is not unusual to find a British burial mound closely connected with Roman remains, Saxon masonry and medieval architecture, and mention is made of another tumulus at High Cross, long believed to be the tomb of one Claudius, leader of a Roman cohort. Further, tumuli between Pailton and Withybrook, and one destroyed by the making of the railway line at Wolston are suggested as evidence of a link between the Watling Street and the Fosse Way, forming a significant triangle of early occupation with the River Avon. It is certainly noticeable, tracing local tumuli on any Ordnance Survey map, that the lines of such earthworks run diagonally across Warwickshire from north-east to south-east, and that they are roughly parallel to the Fosse Way itself. This may, of course, be more by accident than any significant design, but many have suggested that such invisible "ley lines" imply either the sites of ancient and now lost trackways, such as "Tutbury Lane", which runs from the Avon to Brinklow Heath, or that they echo pagan belief in the harnessing of natural earth energy forces along such man-made connections.

Whether Brinklow Tump is the last resting place of a minor British chieftain, circumvented by the Romans and later owned by an Anglo-Saxon named Brynca, or whether it was indeed, the burial place of Brynca himself, we may never know, as to date the mound remains unexcavated. What does seem likely is that there was some form of settlement or human activity in Brinklow long before the Normans built their castle, and later, their fine church. Modern historical research tends to suggest that our old view of ancient Middle England as a vast tract of impenetrable forest is wrong, and that the land, from ancient times, was settled, and even farmed, if in smaller and more isolated communities than exist today.

It is also possible that the present church of St. John stands on the site of a much older sacred place, giving way with the coming of Christianity to an earlier church or chapelry, perhaps Saxon, although it must be said, no evidence of this has yet been found. It is known that Christian churches of great age were invariably established on sites of importance to local communities, often superimposing the Christian ethic on an earlier, pagan one. Mounds, especially burial mounds, were often associated with earth and fertility rites, the midsummer solstice being of particular significance. In the Christian Church, Midsummer Eve, the Summer Solstice, is also St. John's Eve.

Perhaps as a concession to an ambivalent flock, early church builders often incorporated inescapable symbols of the old religion into the fabric of their buildings, and Brinklow Church is no exception - defaced figures on pillars close to the present entrance are almost certainly female fertility figures, and around the corner from the clock tower, is a well-preserved "Green Man" head. Such figures in themselves may have been conceived as an awful warning to backsliding parishioners, but their origins lie deep in the pagan past.

That the Romans themselves passed through, and even stayed awhile in Brinklow is evidenced by the finding, in the 1930s of Roman coins behind the school. The Fosse Way, close to the Roman frontier, was essentially a military road, and was originally a link between the frontier forts and the military ports near Exeter, Bristol and Humber. Later, as conquest flourished, and the border moved northwards, it became a vital trade route, a role which it still maintains today.

It is likely that Brinklow Hill provided an alignment point for the Roman road builders, and although no other Roman artefacts have been discovered, the proximity of Brinklow to Tripontium, (Churchover) the Lunt Fort (Baginton), Venonis, (High Cross) and Ratae

Coritanorum (Leicester), suggests that its earliest inhabitants could scarcely have failed to feel the presence of the legions.

In addition to this circumstantial evidence, modern historical thinking is that the oldest unit of land-holding is the parish, and that modern parish boundaries almost always imply the site of lost Roman settlements - we should not forget that the Romans were in Britain for almost 400 years, and that not all of them were soldiers. There is a tendency to think that the history of villages began with the Domesday Book; it did not. Without evidence, the history of Brynca's Low must remain informed conjecture, but nevertheless, the probability is that despite the turbulence of their times, ordinary people have been doing their best to live ordinary lives on this soil since time began.

The history of a village must always be primarily the history of its people. When the first settlers founded a settlement here, they must have noted its fertile soil, its sheltered aspect - it has often been said that Brinklow has its own climate - and the ready accessibility of ground water, without which they could not have survived. Perhaps those first homesteads were scattered, or grew from a single adventurous family; it may even be that the Hill first drew them as a meeting place, and became their defence. It is possible, even probable, that different communities settled, at different times, until, perhaps, having claimed the land by name, Brynca's people stayed. Over the centuries, the village has seen many changes, as one would expect. The remarkable thing, however, is how much has not changed. The fields, the hill, the road, and Brynca's people endure. This is their story.

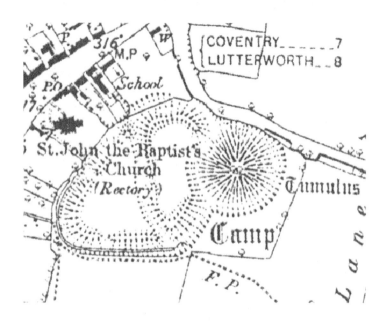

19th century map showing the Norman Castle and its proximity on rising ground to the Church, the school and the Fosse Way. Note the unusual double bailey (Courtyard fortifications) whose impressive earthworks can be seen today. The view from the top of the Motte is spectacular.

Brinklow, from the church tower, looking south.

Brinklow Tump, showing the elm trees that once flourished on top.

Brinklow Castle

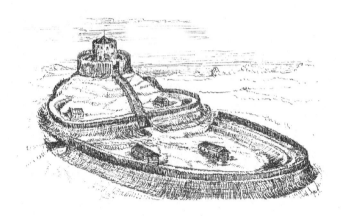

*Brinklow Castle showing the motte and double bailey –
artist's impression.*

The Norman Conquest was a brutal and violent
takeover of an already settled and efficiently
functioning country; in only 20 years between 1066 and
1086, events could not have progressed from conquest
to consolidated military and political power otherwise.
The native English, (despite Norman propaganda to the
contrary) were well organised and effective
administrators; William took over a country in which
trained officials already managed local and central
government, where taxes were collected and where
every village belonging to a hundred had a court which
met every four weeks. Once the country had been
subjugated, and that subjugation enforced by military
might, it was a relatively simple matter to assess and

collect the new rich pickings of the Norman aristocracy through the Domesday survey.

In shape, Brinklow, pre-conquest, was probably very much the way it is today, some habitations spread thinly along the Fosse Way, scattered farmsteads leading to Lower and Upper Smite, (Coombefields) and large open fields and common grazing spread around Brinklow Hill. Before the conquest, the now lost village of Smite was held freely from Edward the Confessor by a man called Harding, who presumably held Brinklow also. The name Harding is comprised of two Old English elements, *heorde* meaning herder, or cattle farmer, and *ing,* meaning "people of"; thus it seems likely that cattle, then as now, were an important part of the Brinklow landscape, and that some, at least, of Harding's people were livestock farmers. There would have been substantially more woodland than there is today, although by no means the heavy forestation of popular imagination; much had already been cleared and cultivated for agriculture.

In 1086, Smite was being managed for the king by Geoffrey de Wirce, a powerful Norman noble with holdings in Warwickshire and Leicestershire. Brinklow is not mentioned in the Domesday survey by name, but Smite is recorded as having land and ploughs for some 47 families, a rather larger figure than one might expect, and Brinklow was almost certainly a populated hamlet of the then larger settlement. It is not unusual for established communities to be missing from the Domesday Book; the survey was purely a tally of assets, and not in any sense a census or parochial record.

There is some evidence that Brinklow already existed as a community in its own right before the Domesday survey, with enough souls to warrant a chapel, albeit an offshoot of "Peterchurche", the mother church of Smite. Smite lay where Coombefields exists today, and its smaller hamlet of Upper Smite can still be traced in the form of grassed earthworks behind Nettle Hill. Peter Hall, now a private residence in Coombfields contains the remains of Peterchurch, some as late as the 13th century. Smite Brook today defines the present boundary between Brinklow and Withybrook, and the lost village itself is remembered in the still extant name of Smeaton Lane. The modern spelling probably echoes the ancient pronunciation; Smite was almost certainly pronounced locally as "Smeet", (Germanic Schmidt),and "Smeaton" the oldest form of the name, stemming from the two Old English elements *smith* meaning worker in metal,and *tun*, meaning farm or village (as in modern "town").

This last throws into question the local legend that Smite (with its connotations to being "smitten") was depopulated as the result of an outbreak of plague, and named in consequence of this seeming demonstration of the wrath of the Almighty. The probable truth is more prosaic. Early in the 11th century, Samson d'Aubigny gave both Peterchurch and "the chapelry of Brinklow" to Kenilworth Priory, who in turn gave or sold it to the Cistercian monks of Coombe, who by 1150 were granted by one Richard de Camville "all my lands of Smite." As wool became the growth industry of the time, the monks of Coombe, as other great landowners elsewhere, needed ever more land for sheep pasture. The cottagers of Smite were almost certainly simply turned out of their homes to provide grazing for sheep. Brinklow grew to its medieval eminence as a result of Smite's misfortune, so in that sense, Smite may indeed be said to have been "smitten".

This wouldn't have been an issue in the closing

years of the 11th century however, in the troubled reign of King Stephen, when the manor of *Brinchelawa, Brinchelau,* or *Brynceslawe* was in the hands of the powerful baron Roger de Mowbray, who held it from the Earls of Leicester. Possibly to settle wrangles about its tenantship by a show of force, or at least to emphasise Norman control over the surrounding countryside, Brinklow Castle was constructed. Castles, in the newly conquered country were the major instruments of subjugation, and Brinklow's fine motte and bailey earthworks, both large and exceptionally well-preserved, are notable for their twofold bailey, surely a sign that the castle was envisaged as a very strong defensive unit.

Wherever there were pockets of rebellion, or reluctance to pay dues exacted, the Normans erected their fortifications. The land around the castle would be cleared of brush and woodland which might offer cover for potential enemies, and even houses were demolished if this impeded the view. The building of castles, firstly in wood, and later in stone, was a massive exercise in forced labour by the local community, so we can be sure that the peasant farmers of Brinklow were first menaced, and later coerced into constructing the castle which once dominated the village from Brinklow Hill.

Brinklow Castle, an early example of Norman fortification, would have been constructed of timber, and was probably in use only for a relatively short time; no trace of stonework has ever been found. Its very existence, however, implies that the Normans felt the area was strategically important, and anyone who today scrambles up the hill on a clear day to marvel at the impressive view of the surrounding countryside, cannot fail to understand why this particular site was chosen.

Castles were constructed first by enlarging existing mounds, or creating new ones, the earth thrown up by digging the moats and ditches being used to heighten the mound and ramparts. The Brinklow castle mound rises some 40ft. above the natural rise of the land, and about 60ft. above the bottom of the moat, which is approximately 40ft. wide, and some 20 ft. deep. The outer bailey was higher by some 10 or 20 ft. than the inner courtyard, and would have been crowned by an imposing wooden palisade - strong pointed stakes used in a close defensive row. A second ditch and rampart would have separated the inner from the outer bailey. On top of the mound would have been a watchtower, reached by a ladder, which in dire emergencies, would have been used as a last refuge, and almost certainly there would have been some kind of drawbridge between mound and outer ditch, supported on two, or perhaps three wooden tiers.

Recent research has suggested that in many cases, prefabricated components for such castles were often brought by sea to England from Normandy, although clearly this may have been influenced by whether the castle was built as a matter of national fortification, or as is most likely the case in Brinklow, as a means of intimidation between localised feuding barons.

Recent excavation of similar motte and bailey sites show that such castles contained a teeming mass of activity - stables, smithies, barracks and fighting platforms jostling for space with all those other buildings necessary to enable an army of occupation to live, eat and sleep beneath the same roof, and, if called upon, to withstand siege conditions. At times of danger, cattle and those local peasants under the protection of the Norman overlord would be driven into the inner bailey, and the outer ramparts manned for defensive action. There are no records to tell us what skirmishes, if any, occurred in Brinklow, and as it seems the castle was abandoned at a relatively early stage, clearly the area soon settled down to some kind of grudging co-existence with the conquerors.

The feudal system continued long after the conquest, and was very complex, largely a story of powerful warring barons, great absentee landowners, tenants-in-chief, and sub-tenants, and the rearranging of landholdings through political marriages and complicated bequests. For the humble cottager, the true inhabitants of Brinklow, with only a subsistence interest of land, or even none at all, life very probably carried on much as it had always done; the intricacies of the lives of their overlords would have meant little other than that their taxes were paid to different people. Of course, some lords were more exacting and others more lenient, but in general, few men were personally free, some were free in name only, bound by the weight of their dues, and others were little more than slaves.

In 1106, the manor of Brinklow passed from Roger de Mowbray to William de Stutteville, and in 1218, his nephew, Nicholas de Stutteville was confirmed in possession by the king. In addition, he was given the right to hold a weekly market on Mondays, and an annual fair on St. Margaret's Day. In 1275, the Earl of Leicester held a court in Brinklow twice a year, and an Assize of Bread and Ale, at which the statuary price of both were fixed.

At the time of the Domesday survey, that part of Warwickshire bordering Leicestershire and Northamptonshire was divided into three "hundreds", or administrative districts. Of these, *Bomelau*, the northernmost, which incorporates Brinklow, seems to have had its centre and court at Brandon (also possessed of a castle) at a place called *Bumbelowe* in 1313, but now another lost village. Later, the same court clearly shifted to Brinklow, and the hundred took its name, functioning as a "leet" (minor court) until the end of the 16th century, although Brinklow, Marton and Stoneleigh were already combined administratively under the name of "Knightlow". To this day, an obscure forfeiture known in 1236-7 as the "warth penny", in 1628 as "the wroth monies" and now as the "wroth silver", is collected from parish representatives at dawn on St. Martin's Day (11th November) on Knightlow Hill (in Ryton-on Dunsmore); Brinklow's tithe, if any, is not recorded.

It would seem, then, that Brinklow had its moment of medieval importance, when, probably due to its position on the Fosse Way, it acted as a centre for trade and jurisdiction. It would have been a thriving, bustling place on those days designated for markets or meetings, and well known in the vicinity. During archaeological excavations before the building of Chandler's Row, amongst evidence of a medieval tannery were found fragments of 13th century Chilvers Coton pottery, providing further evidence of habitation and commerce. There seems to have been a moment in time when it was poised to become a small market town or to slip back into village status. We can still find echoes of that time in Town Yard, between the former Wilkins garage, now the Victorian Ironmonger's, and The Raven Inn, where there were cottages at one time, and in the remaining stretches of the village green, fronting The Crescent.

Brinklow, with its prematurely vacated castle and later its fine Norman church probably fared no worse, and possibly even a little better than most settlements. The early years after conquest may have been ones of repression and stern unbending rule, but the plus side of Norman government was the eventual restoration of order, and a status quo which, if not initially entirely acceptable, became at least stable. Rural life, with its rhythms of the seasons, its periodic disasters in the form of poor harvests and epidemics, its small internal wrangles and its regular communal celebrations probably changed very little until the 17th century, when civil war and religious dissention were to cause an upheaval every bit as great as anything that had gone before.

19th century sketch of Brinklow Hill showing houses in Town Yard

Brinklow looking north from the Church tower

Cottage on the corner of Ell Lane showing the Church

The Church of St. John the Baptist

The Church of St John circa 1820

It seems likely that there has long been a site of some religious or sacred significance where the Church of St. John the Baptist stands in Brinklow today. Although there are no records of an earlier church, the very name of Brynca's Low suggests an Anglo-Saxon presence locally. Modern research suggests that far from falling into disuse after the withdrawal of Roman rule, the great Roman roads such as the Fosse Way actually guided the settlement of incoming Angles and Saxons, and the proliferation of place-names locally with the

Old English suffix *ton* strongly reinforces this. In addition, the pattern of distribution of pagan burial sites and cemeteries, the most striking evidence for Anglo-Saxon settlement, closely coincides with Roman roads and Romano-British settlements.

Originally, the invading newcomers were pagan, but by the end of the 6th century, had converted to Christianity. These early Christians built small wooden churches to serve their spiritual needs, often on pagan sites, and sometimes to serve both as places of worship and as refuge and sanctuary in times of attack. It seems entirely possible that just as the Normans exploited the existing mound for their castle, they may well have sited their church in Brinklow on similarly established religious foundations.

The earliest records state that Brinklow was a chapelry of Smite, and as such, was given to the Augustin Canons of Kenilworth Priory early in the 11th century by Samson D'Aubigny. The original stone church of Brinklow was built by Kenilworth Priory around 1252, the first date we have for a Rector. He was one Hugo de Underwood, and the patronage of Brinklow continued with the Augustin Canons until 1539, when Henry VIII dissolved the monasteries at which time the patronage passed to the Crown. Thus Elizabeth I was the first Royal patron, (followed in the 18th century by the Lord Chancellor, who remains Patron today). The church then had a north aisle, and was built following the contours of the natural slope with a most attractive and rare sloping nave.

The 13th century church probably represents the point in history when Brinklow was poised to become either a thriving market town or remain a village. In 1218, there was a charter granted to hold a weekly market and an annual fair on St. Margaret's Day (July

20th.) and in 1340, a further Grant was made to enable Brinklow to hold another weekly market on Tuesdays. However, perhaps due to the troubled times of that century, with the Black Death raging and civil disturbances such as those that led to the Peasant's Revolt in the next century, the moment passed, and Brinklow was destined to remain a comparatively small community. Fortunately, perhaps due to its position on what must always have been a prominent line of communication, it was spared the fate of many communities such as Smite itself and Hopsford, which are now no more than names on the map, and to this day it has remained a "living" village.

In the 14th century, there were clearly sufficient souls, and Brinklow was a thriving enough settlement for the Prior and Convent of Kenilworth to decide to modernise its church. The present tower was built at this time, and also the south porch (now the vestry), which seems originally to have had a thatched roof. The "perpendicular" style of architecture, much of which remains today, dates from that time, with some larger windows and new roof arches being installed. The windows on the north side of the church are probably the earliest remainders of the old church, as are parts of the north aisle walls. As late as 1500, worshippers in Brinklow would have entered through the south door, and stepped onto an earthen floor covered with rushes. Seating was around the walls, which were decorated with paintings, and the east end of the church was hidden by a large wooden screen, over which ran a gallery. The monks had their own door to the chancel, where the present door is today, and the services would have been in Latin.

After the dissolution, and Henry VIII's break with the Church of Rome, much of the earlier ornamentation would have been stripped away; the wall paintings were whitewashed over and the statues removed. At this time, Kenilworth was said to receive 26s 8d for an annual tithe from "Brinkelowe". The Bible and the services were translated into English for the first time, and the keeping of the church registers was made obligatory. Brinklow's registers date from 1557 for baptisms and burials, and a few years later for marriages; the early ones, beautifully kept, are now held in Warwick Record Office. It should not be thought, however, that worship in Brinklow suddenly became very different; much of the traditional Catholic service would still have been in use, and indeed, during the reigns of Protestant Edward VI, Roman Catholic Mary I and Elizabeth, the momentous affairs of state taking place elsewhere probably affected the ordinary inhabitants of Brinklow very little. Their chief concerns after the spiritual health of their souls was almost certainly the weather, the season and the harvest.

We may assume, however, human nature being what it is, opinion was divided as to the changes, and certainly it soon became impossible not to take sides in the issue of religion. In 1642, Civil War broke out in England, and Warwickshire fell early to the Parliamentary forces. It must have been a time of great upheaval in both county and village alike. The Puritans were zealous reformers, believing that ornament and decoration in churches distracted worshippers from a true contemplation of God. At this time, many of Brinklow's church treasures disappeared, or were damaged, as much through neglect as deliberate intent. The then rector, William Clerke, was summarily removed from office, and replaced by Simon Dingley and John Gilpin, ministers of Puritan persuasion.

The authorities of Oliver Cromwell took religion

very seriously, and attempted to improve the nation's moral health through legislation. Anything thought to encourage licence was banned. Theatres were suppressed as instruments of the devil, maypoles were taken down and forbidden as echoes of pagan fertility rites, and thus encouragements to the sins of the flesh (which, to be fair, they probably were), and then, as now, the demon drink was held to be the cause of loutish, unmannerly, and even sinful behaviour. The following revealing glimpses of Brinklow life are extracted from the records of Warwick Quarter sessions during Parliamentary rule:

EPIPHANY 1652: on proof made in court that Thomas Pagett, John Cotton and Hugh Damford keeping victualling houses in Brincloe are disordered and keep not the assize and also suffer drunken lewd persons to be drinking and tippling in their houses on the Lord's Day and at other times, whereupon it was prayed that they might be suppressed from the selling of ale and victualling, which this court thought fit and doth order the same accordingly.

Given the probable size of Brinklow at the time, seven does seem rather a lot of alehouses, although the image of the village as a hotbed of vice and depravity must be tempered by the Puritans' somewhat dour view of anything enjoyable! It should be remembered that the brewing of ale had a long and respectable history that it was often safer to drink than plain water before the days of universal sanitation, and that formerly, every housewife with a reputation to maintain made the brewing of ale part of her wifely duties.

Equally, those engaged in strenuous agricultural

work might well be excused for having thirsts relative to their labours. That said, amongst a community with its fair share of poverty and distress, perhaps we should not blame the Puritan authorities too much for trying to limit the amount of alcohol consumed by the "children and servants" of "the most substantial inhabitants". It is possible that the name of The Half Moon and Seven Stars, a public house in Brinklow until the 1950s,and still remembered in the name of flats at the lower end of Broad Street commemorates this suppression of six out of seven alehouses.

Clearly the task of administering parish affairs was often a thankless and unpopular one; the records of Warwick Quarter Sessions for the period offer several instances of parish officers neglecting their duty, avoiding their appointments (for which they were nominated rather than volunteering) and sometimes even appearing to cook the books. In 1654, after reprimanding Richard Cure and William Smyth of Coombe for failing to collect 2s. 6d. from the lordship of Coombe for the poor of Brinklow, the court ordered that they collect both the levy and the arrears, and "not to fail, or they will answer to the contrary". At the same time, some discharged their responsibilities faithfully, and showed due concern for the aged and impoverished: in 1665, for instance, both Abraham Fretter and Elizabeth Blake, the first an impotent old man "near fourscore years", and the second "an ancient inhabitant of Brincklow", were allowed to stay in their condemned cottages "without further interruption" in the form of maintenance orders.

With the Restoration of Charles II in 1660, William Clerke was reinstated as Rector, and one is tempted to imagine that many in the village heaved a sigh of relief. The Clerkes were a wealthy landowning family, restoring much of the damage to the church at their own expense, and some celebrations previously banned were restored to favour. The only evidence of Brinklow's Parliamentary past lives on in the name of "Cromwell Cottages", and the legend that the man himself once stayed in the village. He could not have stayed in the buildings that bear that name today, because they are of a later date, but it is entirely possible that earlier dwellings on the site were named during his rule.

Between 1680 and 1743, an astonishing 54 years, the Rector of Brinklow was Thomas Muston. At this time, church seating took the form of "box" pews, most of which were rented by the more substantial citizens; the poor would have had forms to sit on, or would have been forced to stand. The "Reading Pew" and the "Clark's Pew" covered the right -hand side of the present chancel, and the pulpit lay behind, against the pillar. Over the west of the nave was a small musicians' gallery, reached by a spiral staircase, and in common with other villages, Brinklow almost certainly had its own group of ecclesiastical bandsmen, amateur but devoted musicians, playing a variety of instruments not now associated with church music - strings, woodwind, perhaps even a cornet. Early in the 18th century, a chalice and paten, made in London in 1761, were added to church artefacts, and five of the church's six bells were recast at Handsworth, Birmingham; as well as calling the faithful to church, one in particular would have tolled a passing bell for every departed Brinklow soul. This latter bears the sobering inscription:

My Mournfull sound doth warning give that heare men cannot always live".

The Rector between 1793 and 1840, another long period in office, was Richard Rouse Bloxham, sometime Under-master at Rugby School, and father of Matthew Holbeache Bloxham, noted antiquary and historian, Andrew Bloxham, botanist and later Rector of Harborough Magna, and John Rouse Bloxham, originator of the ceremonious revival in the Church of England . Between 1861/62, under the tenure of the Reverend J.C. Ritson, much of the church interior was remodelled at a cost of £850, including a new high chancel arch, and the accentuation of the slope to the nave. New pews were installed on a new wooden floor, and in this era of preoccupation with the social order, the chancel seats were reserved for the more well-to-do members of the congregation, who had the former priests' door as their own private entrance.

Early in the 19th century, the then Curate was instructing around 100 children in the church; in 1826, £100 was raised by private subscription, and a school building consisting of two small classrooms with galleries and a bell turret was erected. Later, around 1871, following the 1870 Education Act, the National Society took over the maintenance of the school, which was also allowed a government grant, provided it followed certain guidelines including the keeping of proper registers and log-books, and allowed regular inspection by government inspectors (often appointed from local clergy.) Brinklow School log-books date from 1871, and the Reverend Ritson's presence is very much in evidence in the early entries, clearly taking a strong interest in educational and social matters, and visiting almost every day.

In 1873, the church organ was donated, and in 1874, the west window, by Mr. Edward Wood of Newbold Revel, who was then manager of the Daimler Motor

Company. It is on record that Mrs. Wood attended church in a flowing purple gown, and was evidently a most charitable woman; members of the congregation would often find packets of tea in the pews, and the organist would discover a £1 note on his stool.

The churchyard contains some very ancient tombstones, amongst which the most unusual bears an epitaph to a deaf and dumb woodcutter, Thomas Bolton of Coombe Fields who died in August 1779. It shows the tools of his trade and the following verse:

He chiefly got his livelihood
By faggoting and felling wood.
Till Death, the conqueror of all
Gave the feller himself a fall.

Nearby, also showing the tools of his trade, is the grave of John Blakemore, maltster and brickmaker, who died in 1820. In 1884, space in the churchyard permitting no more burials, Brinklow Cemetery was opened, the first burial attended by "many people" is recorded as that of "Old John Moore".

Circa 1920: It looks as if the children have just been let out of school

The church has been repaired many times, and will always be in need of some restoration. During this century, coke stoves and oil lamps have been replaced with electricity, and in 1968, the wooden floors of the nave and chancel were renewed. The Chapel of Remembrance of All Souls was dedicated and restored to use in 1969, the gift of Brinklow's branch of the Royal British Legion, who previously, in 1952 started the Remembrance Sunday parades, and in 1953, reinstated the ancient tradition of the Wake Sunday Walk.

Brinklow's parishioners have always been, it seems, a sociable crowd. A copy of the Parish Magazine, the forerunner of Round the Revel, dated July 1897, describes Queen Victoria's Diamond Jubilee celebrations in vivid detail. The occasion must have been one to remember, beginning on the Sunday with a peal from the church bells and the raising of the white ensign over the church tower, followed by services attended by "large congregations". The following Tuesday, a national holiday, again began with celebratory bell ringing, which continued at intervals throughout the day. A large dinner for parishioners had been organised, taking place in a tent (made from rick-sheets), consisting of meat, puddings, bread and cake, and tea for the women and children at 4 o'clock, eating in two shifts. After tea, sports took place, with prizes, followed by dancing in the streets. Later in the evening "a general exodus to the Hills began" and a bonfire and fireworks display was enjoyed by "nearly every inhabitant of the village." The outlay of three guineas for fireworks must have ensured a spectacular display indeed. Every child who attended was given a commemorative cup and saucer and generally, "everything passed off pleasantly, with good feeling and concord."

Brinklow Church: List of Rectors, 1252 – 1995

1252	Hugo de Underwood	1611	Frances Rodes
	William de Pontifract	1624	David Stokes
1298	Hugo de Uppewell	1625	William Clerke
1309	John de Poppering	1644	Simon Dingley
1320	John de Horton	1651	John Gilpin
1324	Henry de Halford	1660	William Clerke
1328	Hugo de Stoke	1671	William Bassett
1331	Nicholas de Astelegh	1680	Thomas Muston
	John de Sutham	1734	John Rushworth
1334	Thomas de Banbury	1772	Marmaduke Matthews
1337	Robert de Shakerston	1774	John Garland
1338	Richard de Schareston	1793	Richard Rouse Bloxham

1339	Robert Sarazyn	1840	John Stuart Hodgson
1349	Richard de Shareston	1858	John Ritson
1350	William de Frankton	1893	William Fox
1374	Adam Abbots	1894	Wm. Pilkington Watson
1407	John Stokes	1908	George Allen Dawson
1408	Roger Reygner	1927	Arthur Milner Startin
1455	Thomas Drowth	1931	Thomas William Story
1489	John Parkys	1937	Ralph Donald Wain
1519	John Magriche	1944	Charles Russell Canham
1524	John Williams	1959	Stanley E. C. Whitcombe
1528	Rad Whitehead	1966	Gordon Ewart Cooke
1534	Henry Breton	1975	Anthony Geering
1541	William Harwar	1982	Roger I. S. White
1583	Gervasius Carington	1991	Paul S. Russell
1584	John Bolton		

Brinklow Congregational Chapel

Brinklow Chapel was built in 1818 by Joseph Butterworth, who was MP for Coventry at the time. It was originally intended to serve the dissenting Wesleyan Methodists in Brinklow, but that particular movement did not seem to have been popular in the village at that time, and the chapel was closed. It remained empty and unused until rented by the Independents of Coventry, (later the

Congregationalists) being formally opened for worship by the Rev. John Sibree on October 28th, 1827. In 1855, it was purchased and vested in trustees, and in 1862, the small room at the back was built under the supervision of Mr. J.S. Beamish, the then pastor. At the same time, new pews were installed. As Nonconformity gathered strength in Brinklow, the old chapel proved inadequate, and the first stone of the new one was laid on 16th July, 1914 by Miss Howe. The new chapel was formally opened in October, 1914. The approximate cost of the whole work was £300, much raised by private subscription. The Pastor at that time was the Rev. George P. Hattrell, and the work was carried out by Mr. Joseph Denyer. A manse for the benefit of a resident Minister was purchased in 1927; the house is now Brinklow Post Office.

Although nonconformity was frowned upon and often persecuted before the passing of the Toleration Act of 1689, it is likely that there has long been a dissenting presence in Brinklow, as in most rural communities. What began with a rejection of any state association with religion was fuelled by the often remote influence of some absentee Church of England clergy and the great power of many travelling Nonconformist preachers to speak to the hearts and understanding of the labouring poor, and those of the middle classes who recognised the injustice of social conditions . It was not until 1836 that Superintendent Registrars were empowered to issue licences for marriage in nonconformist churches and chapels, and before that date, legal marriages, apart from Quakers and Jews could only take place under the Established Church. Many dissenting sects established their own graveyards, but this does not seem to have been the case in Brinklow.

In 1912, a Young Women's Guild was held in the Chapel, and the Rugby Advertiser for March of that year records what was evidently a very enjoyable, (and decorous) social evening, with tea in the schoolroom, followed by a concert in the Chapel. The programme shows the difference in social life before the advent of radio and television; people made their own entertainment, and were clearly very good at it. Familiar names still remembered in the village abound in the report, with a duet from the Misses A. Liggins and S. Capel, and recitations by Miss M. Bayliss and Mr. F. Treen, amongst others.

Brinklow Congregational Chapel

Extracts from the Congregational Chapel Minute books 1914-1943

15 Mar 1914   Plan of the new buildings produced and read out.

19 May 1914   Alteration of building scheme from that of schoolroom discussed.

17 Jun 1914   16th July proposed for stone laying ceremony.

25 Jul 1914   Proposed that enlarged photograph of stone-laying be taken, to be kept in chapel as a memento - cost 8s 6d.

Jan 1916   The Rev. Ralph Blake took over as Pastor.

15 Oct 1917   Rev. Blake to work in France for 4 months.

1 Dec 1920   War Memorial Tablet erected.

16 Dec 1927   The Rev. J.W. Vaughan took over as Pastor.

15 Aug 1929   The Rev. Foxton-Jones took over as Pastor.

12 Jun 1931   Installation of Electric light agreed.

17 Dec 1931   Due to *"these hard and difficult days"* a proposed Japanese Sale of work shelved until *"better days"*.

17 Feb 1932   Mrs. Howes, caretaker, asked to *"do her best to get the chapel warmer in view of the electric light which will not be so warm as   the lamps used at present"*.

18 Oct 1933   Vote that *"no kissing games"* be allowed on church premises carried unanimously.

24 Nov 1933   School closed due to outbreak of diphtheria.

Jan 1936   Rev. H.J. Lewis took over as Pastor.

18 Dec 1936   Central heating installed at cost of £97

10s 6d and switched on for the Carol Service.
23 Oct 1943   Mr. Ballard took over as Pastor.

The Primitive Methodists

It isn't known when this strongly evangelical and dissenting strand of Methodism which broke away from the main body in 1811 began in Brinklow, but as long ago as 1826 there was a Meeting House in Broad Street, and evidence that the group retained some strength amongst the local community is evidenced by a tract "The Dying Experience of Mary Harris", edited in 1860 by Thomas Wolfe, of Brinklow, in which he speaks fervently of the deathbed courage and belief of Mary Harris, a local preacher amongst them. In it he recounts her story, told to illustrate the power of prayer, about a young man of Stretton-under-Fosse whose legs had been broken in an accident on the railway, and who through the good offices of the travelling preacher himself, died converted and content. A Directory for 1880 records both Congregational and Primitive Methodist Chapels active in Brinklow. A number of people in the censuses name "lay-preacher" amongst their everyday occupations, clearly very devout, and proud of their evangelical calling. None, however ring across the centuries with quite the extraordinary fervour of James Fitter, 40 years old and born in Brinklow, who in 1841 gave as his sole occupation: *Servant of Salvation,* 24 years before William Booth founded his Army of the same name.

Brinklow School

Brinklow School and Schoolhouse circa 1950. Note the cottages further along.

In 1625 by the will of Thomas Wale, a mercer of London, lands in Brinklow and elsewhere were left to provide for a schoolmaster and usher in Monk's Kirby, in order to establish a free school for the children of that parish, Brinklow and Stretton. In 1762, the Reverend William Fairfax left 100 guineas for the same purpose, as did William Edwards of Coventry in 1789. In the last century, there seem to have been several private schools in the village; Dunsmore House was one, Watson's Cottage another, and the Misses Hurst had a school for eight boys in Loveitt's Farm, but these would largely have been only for the well-to-do, and parents who could afford the fee.

It is also likely there would have been some form of "dame school" in the village at various times, but these were often little more than child-minding establishments, often over-crowded, and run, as the name suggests by elderly ladies with no particular qualification, and sometimes little interest in their charges; sometimes the "dame" was an elderly man, and any education provided would have been minimal. There is also some evidence of a Dissenting School (i.e. Nonconformist) in Brinklow, as a letter from Thomas Bloxham dated 1826 talks of a Meeting House (which was then Primitive Methodist) and mentions that its school had recently closed. Records of the Congregational Chapel often refer to the "schoolroom". Frequently, these early schools were Sunday Schools, although providing a modicum of education in the three Rs, especially reading, for the purpose of studying the Scriptures. Indeed, the provision of universal elementary education grew out of the Sunday School Movement.

In 1826, Brinklow Church decided to build its own school on the present site, the money to be raised by private subscription, again almost certainly to provide the growing numbers of children in the village with enough basic education to enable them to read the Bible and thus cultivate habits of thrift, industry and, it has to be said, a proper recognition of their station in life. Brinklow, in a letter from the Rector dated the same year, is described as "almost entirely composed of agricultural labourers", and "very poor".

At that time, society was run on strongly class-conscious lines, and the "lower orders" were expected to keep their place, and show due deference to their betters. Equally, poverty was widespread, and the horrors of the French Revolution still fresh in people's minds; opinion in the country was divided on the question of education for the poor. Some maintained that large numbers of educated poor people would only fuel aspirations and make them dissatisfied, and thus a social danger. Others believed that by enabling the lower orders to read and thereby absorb the Scriptures, they would realise that their reward for good behaviour would be in Heaven, and become more accepting and docile.

A few who believed in Education for its own sake, were appalled by the social conditions of the poor, concerned by the lawlessness of poor children in the new industrial towns, and recognised that education was the way to build a better society. We have no way of knowing what exactly was the impetus in Brinklow for the building of a school; it almost certainly grew out of a small charitable institution and the Sunday School, and was originally the business of the curate. 1826, however, many years before the Education Act of 1870 made universal education compulsory, is early for a community to establish a school. There appears to have been a tradition of schooling for the poor, and we can perhaps assume that Brinklow's School grew out of genuine philanthropy. The original school, on the site of an old brickyard, consisted of two classrooms, two more were provided under the School Board Act of 1871, and a further one was added later, from which time the first extant log book dates.

Entries in the school log books reflect a great deal of financial hardship, due to the agricultural depression, and the obvious need for all members of a household to earn as soon as they were able, including children. Seasonal events, such as harvest, potato picking, haymaking, and gleaning disrupted school attendance throughout the early years, and even in the early 20th century, Mr. Bill Smith recalls being called out of school to act as "beater" for the local gentry's sport and being kept waiting in the freezing cold whilst they finished their stirrup cup.

Other events, such as a circus in Rugby, primrose picking, and the local Hunt meeting in the village caused absenteeism, as did the many epidemics of infectious disease. The problems of this latter can be traced in the records of parish burials, sometimes through actual entries of causes of death, and sometimes by the sudden increase in child mortality; in 1832 there were four deaths from cholera, in 1837, thirteen people are recorded as dying from smallpox, and many more children died from "fits", probably measles or scarlet fever. All these diseases, plus diphtheria regularly ravaged the community, striking the most vulnerable, the young and the elderly, and recorded deaths probably only represent the tip of the iceberg; many more people than actually died would have been incapacitated during these regular epidemics of illness in the village. School log-books frequently speak of the school being closed due to infectious disease. In 1846, an infant schoolteacher, Sarah Walton, clearly found things all too stressful; she is recorded as having "poisoned herself in temporary insanity", although we do not know for sure that she taught at Brinklow School itself.

Classes were very large, and the schools were arranged in "Standards", often one class being taught in the same room as another. Pupil teachers, older pupils set to pass on what they had learned to younger children, were regularly used, and often their skills lamented upon in the headmaster's logs. The teaching of the three Rs was of primary importance, and the school's ongoing grant from the Government depended on a good performance when the Inspector came on his regular visit to test the children; this led to great pressure on staff, and inevitably to much rote learning rather than true understanding. Despite all these vicissitudes, the school was clearly a successful and, for its time, an unusually caring one; in 1899, the Diocesan Inspector wrote:

"This is really an excellent school, and I do not know that I can give Mr. and Mrs. Nolder too high praise for the very excellent work that is being done not only by themselves but by the whole staff under them.
It is always a pleasure to go to Brinklow school'

In 1871, Mr. William Nolder and his wife Frances were appointed to the school as Master and Mistress, and continued for almost the next 40 years, assisted over that time by a succession of Monitors and Pupil Teachers. Until 1902, children were required to pay "school pence" of around 2d a week, and even this small sum seems to have been difficult for some parents to find. Children started as young as three, and continued until thirteen or fourteen, often leaving well before that to work illegally, or working half time before the legal age. In 1911, Mr. Nolder retired; from what we know of him, he appears to have been stern, sometimes intolerant, and conscientious to the point of despair in many instances. In that, he was no worse, and possibly a little more caring than many for his times.

Mr. Nolder was succeeded by Mr. Frank Gwinn until 1931, who sadly, died in office. Mr. Gwinn was an enlightened man who is remembered by many in Brinklow with affection and respect. Mrs. Denyer became Acting Head, followed by Mr. Tullet(1931-1934), Mr. Hicks (1934-19460,Mr. Philips (1946-1966), Mr Price (1967-1973) Mrs. J. Banks, (nee Peberdy) (1973-1983) Mrs. S. Bond (1984-1988), and Mrs. F. Bennett (May 1988-)

The War Years: 1914-1918

In 1915, children from Brinklow School collected money for Christmas presents to the men overseas, and throughout the war made collections for Sick and Wounded Horses and the Rugby Prisoner of War Fund. A group of children visited Pailton House which was a military hospital at the time, and entertained wounded troops, and the girls knitted for the Red Cross Society. Another project was "Jam for Soldiers", in which 140lbs of blackberries were collected in a single afternoon, and sent as jam to soldiers at the front. The following year, 690lbs were collected and sent. Children also picked primroses, and sold them in Rugby for the War Effort.

1939-1945

Mr. Hicks, headmaster of Brinklow School when war broke out, was also Billeting Officer for evacuees and the school day was altered to accommodate the visitors, some lessons taking place in the Church Rooms. The air-raids on Coventry in 1940 swelled numbers even further, as families came to stay with relatives in Brinklow, bringing their children with them, uprooted, often frightened, and sometimes finding it difficult to settle. For a time, the school was used as an Emergency Feeding store, and officials from the Ministry of Agriculture came regularly to inspect stocks. In 1942, a teacher from the school, Mr. Holt, was killed on active service in Libya.

An Exciting Discovery

In October 1932, the log-book records the finding, by two boys digging in the school bank, of a number of pieces of pottery and two old coins. These were sent to Birmingham Archaeological Society, and the possibility of excavating the Castle was discussed with Major Gregory Hood, Lord of the Manor but was not followed up.

The Adult Schools

From 1910, an "Adult School" was conducted in the village, almost certainly catering for those young people who were too old for primary education, but still under the legal age for full-time employment. The classes, in handicraft and cookery seem to have been held originally in the Church Room, and later in the former candle factory premises, and the idea was not without its detractors. The Rugby Advertiser for February and April of 1912 reports what sounds like a successful venture, with accounts of a "Parish Tea and Limelight Exhibition" for the old people of the village , *"temptingly laden tables"* being followed by a magic lantern show entitled "The Conquest of the Air", and an "Open Sunday" when a collection was made for the survivors of the Titanic shipping disaster.

The school frequently put on fund-raising events for Parish funds, and the scheme's chief supporters seem to have been Councillor and Mrs. Pegg (of Pegg's Cottage), Mr. and Mrs. Peet, and the Misses Manger,

Bateman, Edmunds, Mawby and Dawson. The Advertiser further reports that *"The School Committee worked indefatigably...and set an example which, if followed, would do much to create and develop that mutual goodwill which is so desirable in villages."*

All that said, it is surprising, and a little sad to read on May 12th 1912, of a heated disagreement at a Parish Council meeting in the village, where Councillor Woodward stated that the proposal to rent "Mr. Podmore's factory" at an annual rent of £13, was *"a gross waste of ratepayers' money"*. A Mr. Brown, agreeing, said he thought the class had been unsuccessful, and Mr. Neale seconded the motion, stating that he *"should be sorry to retard the cause of education in the village, but....some effort should be made to check the rapid growth of expenditure"*. The Chairman agreed that he had experienced *"...great difficulty in inducing numbers of students necessary to make these classes possible,"* but referred to the "Continuation School" of the previous year, which had been an unqualified success. One's heart goes out to all those who clearly worked so very hard to foster education for older pupils in the village, and who worked so "indefatigably" to earn approval.

The School seems to have weathered the storms, and many older residents remember receiving lessons in The Candle factory; the late Mrs. Flora Greasley recalled being taught housecraft on the upper floor in the 1920s, told a timeless story of the day she and another girl were set to learn how to scrub a table. There were, she remembers, holes in the floor, through which they could plainly see the boys downstairs doing woodwork, watched, oddly enough, by some geese. Every time the teacher looked away, the young Flora and her friend slopped water through the holes, trying to hit either boys or geese. Times change, but human nature doesn't, it seems, especially that of adolescent girls.

Although mention of the school's *"Second anniversary meeting"* suggests it opened in 1910, the Brinklow Handicraft Centre log books for 1912-1940, in Warwick Record Office, state that a class opened in Brinklow on September 8th, 1912, the teacher being Samuel Cocker. In February 1913, the students were making a large cupboard for the school, being visited by the Headmaster, Mr. Gwinn, and being taught by *"R. Emerson, Young Instructor"*. In October the school was closed due to an epidemic of whooping cough, and only re-opened in December. In January and February of 1940, the school was closed again, due to "severe weather", which sounds as if pupils came from the other Revel villages, and that Brinklow was snowed in. In December of that year, the Adult School was closed for the last time, perhaps with the dire events in nearby Coventry on everyone's mind, work on the land needed more than ever, and the prospect of evacuees to cater for.

Two carved altar crosses and one writing desk were made for St. John's Church by local craftsmen: Dennis Baker, Henry Bachelor, and Sam Mace. It isn't known whether these were made under the auspices of the Adult School, but the young men of the classes were certainly constructing various cupboards and other items for the school at different times.

Circa 1920 Physical Education in the School Yard.

Sadly we have no names for this very early photo, but note the pupil teacher.

Brinklow School, Class 5, 1926

Back L/R: Barbara Bales, Frank Duffin, Donald Wilkins, Tommy Harris, George Hailstone, Willie Brindle, Arthur Hammond, ? Edwards, Freddy Howes, Stan Titcomb, Iris Hickman

2nd Row L/R: Eileen Crawley, Hilda Bachelor, Madge Watkins, Elsie Capel, Edith Colledge, Mabel Hopkins, Mercer Bond, Nancy Jessett, Kath Hailstone, ? Jessie Grindle

3rd Row L/R: Vi Howes, Florence Smith, Phyllis Cox, Betty Denyer, Joan Missen, Dess Denyer, ? Titcomb. Brenda Billington

Home Time 1950's

Brinklow Enclosure Award

Traditional agriculture in the 18th century involved peasants (owner occupiers and tenants farming small areas of land known as strips which were intermixed with those of others in large open fields according to communal agreement. The three fields of Brinklow were named Ell, Brook and Licence. The village also had uncultivated common land, known as commons or waste used for rough grazing, fuel gathering and timber. Brinklow's common land was where the Park is today.

Enclosure was the process by which the various strips of each owner were reorganised into separate holdings, fenced off from the land of their neighbours. Where there were commons, this land too was divided up between those who had rights to use it. The process made agriculture more efficient but it also had a major impact on the communities affected. One consequence was that many small landowners and tenants could not afford the obligatory and expensive fencing demanded and were forced to sell their holdings or vacate their tenancies. They often moved away to neighbouring towns in search of work, as fewer labourers were needed under the new system and this too contributed to a slow but remorseless drift from the countryside.

The process of enclosure generally began by big landowners in a community obtaining a local Act of Parliament. This authorised the appointment of Enclosure Commissioners, local men, one of whom was often a surveyor. They would investigate the rights of each interested party, survey the land, allocate fields and lay out new roads. Their final decision was then embodied in a formal written document, the "Enclosure

Award", which from the later 18th century was usually accompanied by a map. The map for Brinklow has not been found, but the much later Glebe Map is helpful is working out where places might have been. A local copy is in the Church Hall and the original is in Warwick Record Office.

Brinklow's enclosure award gives an overview of the community at a crucial moment in its history. It gives the names of many who owned or occupied land in 1741 and identifies the land which they owned. It some major changes to the landscape and set the scene for how the fields are arranged today. Much however is still there beneath the present day, and with field names and maps we can often see a glimpse of medieval Brinklow.

Plain language summary of the preamble to the award:

I have transcribed the variations in spelling and grammar as they appear in the original. Spelling was very much a matter of personal inventiveness at the time. The original is in Warwick Record Office and is a vast document. Unfortunately the accompanying map seems to have been lost. However maps tended to be hand copied from older ones so later maps are quite helpful. The brackets indicate my explanations.

The findings and instructions of the Commissioners for the Enclosure Act for Brinklow was passed in the 14th year of George II (The year beginning June 1741)

The enclosure of the common fields, pastures, meadows and wastes of Brinklow should be set out and allotted on or before the 25th March 1742 by the Gentlemen Commissioners or any five of them: (The first day of the year 1742, in the old style calendar when the year began in March not January.)

John Lant of Baberley
John Boddington of Whitmore Park
George Worth of Newnham Regis
John Rider of Nuneaton (vicar).
Joseph Parsons of Weston (Bulkington)
Henry Norton of Wicken (Wyken, Coventry)
William Butler of Hundred Oaks
Samuel Barnett of Warwick
Benjamin Clarke of Hardington, Northants

A survey should be made of the land to be enclosed some time before 29th September 1741 to include lot-grass, tying grass, hades and baulks.

(Lot grass refers to land tenured by the drawing of lots, arable or pasture; tying grass is possibly enclosed pasture or land that had tithing or a tax on it; hades were headlands where the plough turned; baulks were strips of uncultivated land acting as boundaries between individual strips, possibly only visible after harvest.)

I) The Glebe Lands (land sublet where rents were allocated to pay the Rector's stipend)
The Commissioners should set out and allot the share for the Rector, John Rushworth and his successors in recompense for the glebe lands that lay in the common fields to a full one tenth of what was to be enclosed to satisfy the tithe apportionments, but in one whole plot in Brookfield as near to the parsonage house as possible. This large plot was to be subsequently divided within twelve months into manageable (farm like and

tenantable proportions or closes) by sound fences, ditches and quickset hedges which were to be maintained and the cost borne by the owners/tenants excepting the Rector himself. The same to be true of the tithe lands lying in Ell and License (the common medieval fields of Brinklow; tithe lands were land where the rent went towards Parish funds to pay for things like the constable, maintenance, and poor relief.)

2) Fulwar, Lord Craven: 12 acres of the waste, more or less, called Mutton Hole next to Birkley's Coppice (Birchley Wood) was to be allotted to the Right Honourable Fulwar, Lord Craven in lieu of his rights over the wastes of Brinklow. Immediately following this, his rights in common pasture in Brinklow should cease and be extinguished as should any rights of freeholders of Brinklow to herbage or pasture in Birkley's Coppice or to watering their cattle in the park and pool of Coombe Abbey. (As they had obviously been used to doing this). Within twelve months the Cottagers of Brinklow should be allotted each an entire plot of land in one of the three fields in exchange for their rights of common and the waste.

The Commissioners were to set out and appoint new public or private roads through the new enclosures so that everyone entitled to pass was able to reach his own lands, nd in order that appropriate fencing etc. be erected calculating the contribution that should be made by the Rector, Fulwar, Lord Craven, the Master fellows and Scholars of Trinity College Cambridge and the Cottagers of Brinklow.

The Commissioners were to put their findings into a written Award containing exact apportionments and instructions for access to the new allotments, plus any extra orders deemed necessary which should be deposited with the Clerk of the Peace at Warwick, and should be available to anyone at any time. This would be a legal document. The area to be enclosed was 1,198 acres, 1 rood and 34 perches.

Although we have no Enclosure Map, the later 1835 Glebe Map in association with a terrier, (list of owners and occupiers,) helps enormously to understand the Award.

For more details of place names see Appendix II.

1940s Ariel photograph courtesy of Brinklow's war hero, the late Mr Reg Cleaver who took the picture. Mr Cleaver was shot down in 1943 near Cologne. He spent five weeks on the run before he was captured by the SS and sent to the Stalag Luft III prisoner of war camp.

This clearly shows the line of the Fosse Way the motte and Bailey to the left of the road and the layout of fields after enclosure. Ridge and furrow farming shadow is clear in the right foreground.

Brinklow Canal

ENLARGED PART OF BRINKLOW PARISH

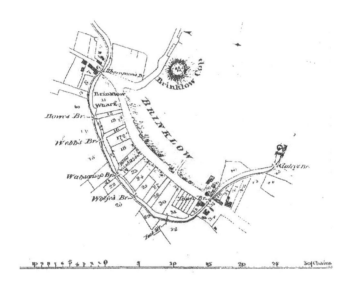

The map shows where the canal entered and left Brinklow passing behind the Crescent and part of Broad Street.

On 18th August, 1766, a public meeting at Warwick considered proposals to build a canal from the Trent and Mersey to Coventry, and an extension of the Oxford Canal. The Coventry Canal was agreed upon, and work proceeded, but the Oxford proposal was temporarily shelved. However, on 25th October, 1766, the engineer James Brindley submitted a report and survey for the Oxford Canal at a public meeting held at the Three Tuns in Banbury. £50,000, an astonishing sum for the time, was subscribed on the spot. The commercial impetus for such a waterway was partly to join the River Thames, and thereby to gain access to London, but perhaps more importantly, stemmed from Oxford and Banbury's need for coal from the Midland coalfields.

An Act of Parliament for the Oxford Canal had been passed in April, 1769, but a clause was inserted prohibiting carriage of any coal beyond Oxford. Work began almost immediately, and by 1772, the first ten miles of canal from Longford Junction to Brinklow was completed. In that year, James Brindley died, and Samuel Sibcock succeeded him as engineer. Brindley, however had been responsible for the deeply curving contour course and for the design of Brinklow Aqueduct, a major feat of engineering, having twelve arches, each of a 22ft. span.

At Banbury, the work stopped when the company faced financial difficulties, partly due to the war with America, but by 1790, work continued to Oxford. The cost of the initial stretch to Banbury, nearly 64 miles, was £199,304, and the total cost to Oxford was £307,000. The entire canal was open by 1794, the main cargoes being coal iron, corn, copper, chemicals, cotton and Irish linens.

The contour line of the original Oxford canal meant that it was never truly competitive. It took a whole day, for instance, to go through Brinklow, crossing the main road twice, once between where Carlton House now stands and the iron gates opposite, running behind The Crescent and Broad Street, and again, back through Dock Yard, originally a mooring for the building and repair of boats, and across the road past Harmony Farm; very useful for local publicans, no doubt, but bad for the carriage business. Competition from the newly burgeoning railways and various improvements to the Birmingham Canal put the Oxford Canal Company again at severe financial risk, and so, in 1829, it was surveyed for straightening. Around 1831, John Ferguson, (who later built Carlton House) was appointed resident engineer, and the new, more direct stretch was opened in 1834.

Although by that date, Brinklow had lost its through canal, the quarter-mile Brinklow Arm remained in use as a wharf until the 1920s, and some local women still wore the traditional large "boatee" sunbonnet. A loading wharf was near to Dove House Farm, and behind The Rise was once a depot for coal, bricks, pipes, tiles, fodder and cattle requirements. The Brinklow Arm was clearly used for pleasure boating as the following delightful extract from the Rugby Advertiser 7th July 1857 reports:

"....an aquatic party, per canal from Coventry with a brass band ended their day thus: as the sun sank in the far West the happy couples wended their way to the Fair Rosamund, which was moored off "Brinklow Bay...."

It is very probable that some of the houses between Carlton House and Dock Yard were built with the expectation of increased commercial prosperity for Brinklow with the opening of Brindley's canal. Post Office Yard, for instance, extends to, and crosses the site of the defunct arm, and a brick building at the bottom of the yard is one quarter of a once much larger building, probably a warehouse on the far side of the canal. Nos. 11 and 13. The Crescent, built circa 1780 were originally one house, and the vast cellar beneath what was Brinklow Pottery, much larger than one would expect in an ordinary dwelling of the era, suggests that the property was always commercial in nature, almost certainly a provisioning stop for boats on the canal.

The 1834 map of Brinklow canal shows that there were originally eight bridges over the canal from its entry into Brinklow at Thompson's Bridge on the Lutterworth Road to Cluley's Bridge behind the White Lion. Most of these were named for local people, those over whose land the bridge passed, or those who most used it; Howe's Bridge clearly being named for the family who later developed the candle factory in Brinklow, Webb's Bridge after the landowner Hannah Webb, Wolfe's Bridge after Thomas Wolfe, interestingly both local preacher and licensed victualler and William Cluley, licensee of the White Lion. Although the canal had gone long before present living memory, many older villagers can remember the traces of those bridges and the deep holes that filled with water where it once crossed the village. The canal gave much needed employment to many local villagers, and some families have a colourful family history showing births and baptisms along the whole stretch of canal villages between Hawksbury and Leicestershire; wives of "boatees" frequently lived and worked alongside their families.

James Brindley's canal arches were an engineering marvel. Though overgrown they are still visible in Brinklow.

House History: Carlton House

It is not yet known where John Ferguson, resident engineer of the Oxford Canal, lived initially, but the Brinklow census of 1841 records him as living with his wife, Mary, on the north-west side of the turnpike road from Coventry; Carlton House, the imposing blue-brick building on the left hand side going towards Lutterworth, which he subsequently built at least before 1876, stands on the line of the disused canal, and accords with the description, so was very probably built between 1834 and 1841. An extract from the deeds of Carlton House records it as being *"one rood or thereabouts....having stable and coach house, and other buildings known as the Old Mill..."* (now Nutwood Cottage).

Parish records for Brinklow record that John Ferguson died August 10th 1854 aged 69, and his wife Mary on 14th March 1862, aged 84. Both are buried in Brinklow Churchyard - the grave is found by going left of the main doorway of the church, up the slope to the back corner, and is a large tomb surrounded by iron railings. Mary Ferguson, in her will of 1862, bequeathed to the rector and churchwardens of Brinklow a substantial sum of money, the interest amounting to £2 12s od to be given amongst deserving widows of the parish at Christmas; this charity is still in operation.

It has been suggested that at one time, Carlton House was owned by the Suttons of Sutton Stop (Hawksbury Junction), and that a Sutton married a Spencer of the Coventry ribbon-weaving family, a relative of David Spencer, Nonconformist Congregationalist, an extremely wealthy ribbon manufacturer, who gave Spencer Park to the City of Coventry. There is certainly a record of a marriage between a David Spencer and a Tabitha Sutton on 24th January 1831 at Foleshill, although this family does not appear in the 1841 census for Foleshill. In the 1851 census for The Canal Stop, Foleshill, however, a Henry Sutton, aged 45, and born at Stretton appears as the canal toll-clerk, living with his wife and family. This Henry appears in the 1861 census at Hawksbury Stop, and in the 1871 census for Brinklow (address not recorded) as a farmer of 87 acres employing 2 men and a boy.

Henry Sutton would seem to be the son of Richard Sutton, who was appointed canal clerk in 1807, and from whom Sutton Stop gained its local name, still in use today. Both were buried at the United Reform Church, Old Church Rd. Coventry, so it may be that Henry Sutton retired to Brinklow to farm, perhaps moving into Carlton House itself, but returning to Foleshill as his final resting-place. The parish records for Stretton-under-Fosse record a Sutton family baptism in Sept. 1797 and marriages in 1832, 1843 and 1849, although as yet, Henry Sutton's baptism has not been discovered.

Subsequent owners/occupiers of Carlton House were:

1896:	Mrs. Whalley
1900:	Miss Bate
1921:	Miss Ingram (teacher)
1928:	Miss Ingram
1940:	Mr. Charles Tew

Chapman's Factory, making electrical parts, occupied the site of Nutwood Cottage during World War II.

Carlton House.

Transport and Communication

Evidence of the early work of Wilkins Garage, which moved with the times and went from making halters and saddles to working with bicycles and dispensing petrol.

Brinklow has always been a large village; in 1730 there were about 100 houses, containing an estimated 300 head of population per square mile, almost as large as nearby Bulkington, and in 1871 there were 810 residents. Its unusually wide village street, formerly known as Main Street was once cobbled, and in the 18th century, its upkeep was taken over by a Turnpike Trust, and toll gates were installed at both ends of the village. As a major route, the Fosse Way was an important coaching road, and several of the inns were also coaching inns where horses could be changed and travellers obtain refreshments. Crook House and Yard was once one such coaching station, as were also The Bull's Head and the now defunct The Dun Cow where now new houses stand.

Local transport for the more humble villagers was available at a much lesser cost by carrier and cart, and a network of such carriers plied regularly between all local villages and towns. In 1866, the carrier was John Bachelor, and the Bachelor family were still carriers in Brinklow until the 1930s. By 1940, The Midland Red Motor Omnibus passed through the village on Saturdays and Sundays.

Many local people had their own horse drawn transport, and others could hire a wide range of small and large equipages; the notes of the Misses Cryer recall tandems of horses, large and small brakes, London Cabbies, landaus, broughams and flies in regular use from William Rowe of The Bull's Head, listed in an 1896 Directory for Brinklow as a "Horse trainer". Older residents remember Miss Howe, who ran a school from Dunsmore House, driving her donkey cart along the Coventry Road. Wilkins Garage, next to the Raven Inn, and now a private house was originally a saddlers, and Mr. Burdett Wilkins was noted for making horse collars, an interesting example of a local business moving with the times.

Brinklow Station

Brinklow Station (actually at Stretton) was opened before 1866, and was in full use until the "Beeching axe" of the 1950s. Extracts from Mrs. Friswell's diary, dated 1886 show that the service was much appreciated by the villagers

"....Sept 20th...An excursion trip train called at Brinklow Station for the London Exhibition. Many people joined it..."

In March 1912, The Great Central Railway Company were engaged in negotiations on the subject of building a branch line from Coventry to Lutterworth, connecting up the villages on the route. The idea was viewed with enthusiasm by Brinklow Parish Council, on the grounds that it would enable workers to come and live in the country and also, that it would make it easier for villagers to work in the growing town. The only problem, as Councillor Neal saw it was that the moment wasn't opportune, due to "the calamitous coal-strike". The line was also envisaged as facilitating the development of the mineral wealth of the area, gravel, and possibly coal, and so hopes were high. The project, however, foundered with the outbreak of war, the moment passed, and it was never revived again. Brinklow was thus saved from the fate of other industrial villages, and remained relatively unscathed by progress. At its hey-day, eight trains a day ran from Brinklow Station, and a substantial number of Brinklow men are recorded in the later censuses as finding work in portering, plate-laying, and general railway maintenance.

The Telegraph Service came to Brinklow in April 1882, and was *"very busy for local Gentry...especially when Coombe Abbey, Town Thorns, Newbold Revel and Newnham Paddox were in their full glory"* (Miss Cryers' notes,). It was situated at the Post Office, then working from The Half Moon and Seven Stars and employing three full-time telegraph boys working in relays, and walking until bicycles came into everyday use. The Half Moon and Seven Stars clearly had many extra functions in its time; in 1840, The Magistrates met there, and later (probably from 1837) it was used by the District Registrar who attended part-time for the registration of births, marriages and deaths.

Brinklow Station

The Candle Factory

The Candle Factory before its demolition in 1986

Although the date on John Howe's now sadly demolished Candle Factory, formerly behind Tallow Cottage, was 1874, tallow candle making has rather a longer history in Brinklow. The earliest form of candle was made by dipping dried plant stems into tallow (mutton or beef fat), although later, cotton fibres were used for wicks. Until the 18th century, most candles were made by the people who actually used them, and housewives saved fats from the kitchen to make them. Since the beginning of the 19th century however, candle-making on a commercial basis began as a cottage industry, and later took place in factories.

The process involved boiling the tallow with acid-treated water to separate the fat from fibrous matter, then heating it with steam and slaked lime and mixing it with paraffin wax to reduce guttering when lit. It was inevitably a smelly business, and everyone in The Crescent must have been painfully aware of it, although perhaps grateful that it brought much needed work to the village.

In the 1841 census for Brinklow, John Howe, a Brinklow man and his wife Martha, born in Wolvey, were living in The Crescent with their baby son, John, and are recorded as Tallow Chandlers. There is nothing to show that at this time John Howe was a Master Chandler, as several other residents in the village in the same census give the same occupation.

In 1851, there are still some tallow chandlers recorded, but no John and Martha, although an Ebeneza (sic) Howe, book keeper, was living in what seems to be the same address, so perhaps the couple were simply away from home. (An Ebenezer Howe appears on the 1837 Glebe Map, owning land next to that of John Howe, but it doesn't seem to be the same one, although possibly it may be his father or even grandfather.) Certainly in 1861, although John is not present on census night, Martha is, and so is her daughter, another Martha, aged 18, and her son Robert, who is now doing the book keeping. This census shows that by then, John Howe was employing 5 men, 2 women and a boy. The presence of a book keeper suggests that the tallow chandlery was in operation in perhaps a small way back as far as 1851. In that year, there was also a Sarah Howe living in the village, an infant teacher aged 22 and born in Manchester, who may or may not be a relation; she could be John's sister, as the name Sarah does crop up in the family again.

By 1871, John's son, another John, living with his wife Selena and his three children, had already expanded the business to the point where he employed 16 men and occupied 16 acres, so clearly the site of the factory was in use, even if the building that was only demolished in the 1980s had not then been constructed. The first reference in a census to "The Candle Factory" is in 1881, and John, Selina, their children Olive, Annette and Ann, and Ebenezer, now revealed as his cousin, are still living at the site, almost certainly in Crook House, although the house is not named in any census, and its full history remains to be researched.

In 1891, Martha Howe, John's mother and a widow, was living in Dunsmore House with her unmarried daughter Sarah, aged 46, running a private boarding school, and her granddaughter Selina aged 20, clearly the second John's daughter. (Sarah cannot be the same one as the 1851 Sarah, as the ages and places of birth do not tally). Some older residents remember Miss Sally Howe as a somewhat eccentric old lady who made schoolchildren do jobs for her, setting little traps to "test" their honesty by leaving sixpences on the shelf, and driving her donkey cart to Coventry. The donkey, according to Mr. Bill Smith (senior) eventually drowned "in the cut".

There is no mention of the candle factory in the 1891 census, and clearly by then it had closed. In 1912, it belonged to a Mr. Podmore, was disused for manufacture, and was subsequently used as accommodation for the Adult School.

JOHN HOWE,

WAX AND TALLOW CHANDLER,

BRINKLOW, near Coventry,

BEGS to inform the Public that he now Manufactures and has constantly on SALE,

THE IMPROVED OCTAVE MOULD CANDLES.

They give as much light as two common moulds, burn without snuffing, and can be used in the ordinary candlestick.

J. H. begs to apologise to his customers for the unavoidable delay in executing their orders for the IMPROVED DIP CANDLES (which never require snuffing), and takes this opportunity of informing them, that arrangements are now made, which he trusts will prevent any delay for the future.

The Silk Mill

Very few facts are known about the Silk Mill which opened at the lower end of the village on 1st July 1872, other than it was owned by a Mr. Tom Alfred Soden Iliffe, and managed by a William McDonagh. Although both Iliffe and Soden, neither very common surnames, are to be found in Brinklow, neither of the families concerned seem sufficiently wealthy to produce an owner of a business; nevertheless, it seems likely that there was perhaps some family connection. Tom Iliffe certainly owned Brandon Silk Throwing Mills, located on the Wolston side of Brandon Railway bridge and Station, probably acquiring the business at an auction of 1867. In the 1881 census for Ryton on Dunsmore, he is recorded as living at "Mill House, Brandon & Bretford", but in an 1874 directory entry for Brinklow he appears as "Silk Throwster & Brandon Mills", so clearly the Brinklow Mill was an expansion of his other business. In 1881, Tom Iliffe was aged 44 and unmarried, the only other

The Silk Mill was the large building on the left

occupant of the house besides servants, one Arthur Edward Jagger, Silk Broker, aged 30.

An intriguing possibility is that George Kenning, one of the most successful makers of ceremonial insignia in the 1880s was in some way connected with the Brinklow Silk Mill. Ishmael Kenning and his family certainly lived in Mill Cottages in 1881, next door to Mill House, were all throwsters in the silk trade, and it is interesting to note that George Kenning (whose baptism has not yet been located) went into business with Richard Spencer, a member of the illustrious Coventry ribbon-weaving family who also probably had connections with Brinklow through marriage of a Spencer to a Sutton.

In 1956, the firm of Kenning & Spencer was taken over by the firm of Toye and Company, to become Toye, Kenning and Spencer Ltd, one of the biggest manufacturers of Insignia in the country, and by Royal Appointment, suppliers to H.M. The Queen. Ishmael Kenning, whose wife Mary came from Stretton-under-Fosse looks likely to have been George's brother, and both may well have been the sons of another George Kenning, born in Ryton on Dunsmore in 1788.

The Brinklow mill was situated at the Coventry Road end of the village and is now private apartments. A sense of its earlier architecture can still be seen, best from The Bull's Head car park. The main thing we know about the operation of the mill is the problem it caused for Mr. Nolder, Headmaster of Brinklow School. For some time before the mill opened, outworking was going on in villagers' own homes, the knotting of fringes and trimmings being carried out by women and small children. A good many girls and boys were missing school and working under-age in the "Wrighton" Silk Mill, (clearly Iliffe's mill), and the attendance became so poor that Mr. Nolder wrote to the Factory Inspector, who promised to rectify the situation.

Immediately the Brinklow mill opened, attendances dropped even more alarmingly. This was not only a matter of concern to Mr. Nolder as a teacher, and a genuinely caring man, it also meant that he was in serious danger of losing the Government grant - grants were conditional on both the number of attendances, and the pupils reaching a certain standard in the three Rs, which plainly they couldn't do if they were working, or if they were so tired they fell asleep. If pupils were missing school or doing badly in tests, he had little chance of impressing the Inspector of Schools, and a bad situation could only get worse.

Children as young as four were employed at home in knotting and fringework, and frequently the mill took on children of ten in deplorable conditions for long hours despite the half-time legal age of twelve. Often, older girls had to mind the youngest children whilst the mother worked at home. We should be careful before we blame their parents too much; after 1860, the import duty on silk ribbons was lifted and the market was flooded with cheap French ribbons; the resulting slump brought much unemployment and increasing poverty to an area where already the call for agricultural labour were beginning to decline. In a way, perhaps it is surprising that Tom Iliffe should have expanded when all the signs for the English silk trade were bad, but for the relatively few years it appears to have lasted, income from the mill must have seemed a godsend to the hard-pressed villagers of Brinklow.

Mr. Nolder, however, clearly beside himself, wrote a stiff letter of complaint to the manager of the Silk Mill. His letter has not survived, but we can guess from the increasing bitterness of the log book entries, and the tone of the Manager's reply, that it was vehement:

Dear Sir,
I did not think that you understood the management of the Silk Mill, or I should have asked you a little advice how I should carry out my trade. I think I can go on without such instruction as you give or if you like to act as certifying surgeon you may come and pass the children every day and I cannot compel him nor you either to come oftener. If you are a School Master, I am Manager of the Silk Mill.
I remain
Yours etc. W. McDonagh.

Of William McDonagh, manager of the Silk Mill, we know little other than he was born in London and married Hannah, a girl from Ryton on Dunsmore. The family clearly lived in Brinklow, as Edward, their son was born there in 1873, three years after the Silk Mill opened, and another son, Elijah was born there in 1877. In 1872, McDonagh would have been 27, and perhaps his indignation concealed uncertainty about his own situation; we do not know exactly how long the Silk Mill operated in Brinklow, but it seems to have closed some time before 1891, when no silk workers appear in the census, probably around 1882, when Mrs. Friswell's diary records a Sale at the Silk Mill.

William McDonagh and his family had left by 1881, and in the census of that year he was living in Coventry in somewhat reduced circumstances and working as a drayman. In addition to all his other worries, the poor man had just become the father of twin girls, so perhaps we should reserve judgement. It is not recorded what Mr. Nolder thought of the matter, but poor attendance at the school continued to harass him throughout his career.

House History: No. 11
The Crescent
(formerly Brinklow Pottery)

Brinklow Post Office and village stores circa 1890

There are no early deeds available for No. 11, The Crescent, formerly Brinklow Post Office, and since 1985, Brinklow Pottery. The story is they were lost in a fire; it remains to be seen if any documentation will ever surface. However, much can be discovered about a house history through other means, and the following record, probably dating from the building of the house has been a matter of detective work, following clues, digging in censuses - such a story will never be completely told - there is always more to find.

The early history of No. 11 is also the history of No. 13, because originally they were one house. It has been suggested that No. 15 was also part of the same dwelling, but although the facade would seem to support the idea, close examination of the back of the houses reveals that No. 15 was in fact built on - the roof and chimneys are quite different. No. 15 was originally the police house, complete with lock-up, but does not appear so in any census; an early photograph clearly shows the Police plaque still on the house however. The front of the three houses was clearly refaced at some time, and the cladding bricks stop just round the corner in Post Office Yard (formerly Cleaver's Yard).

The earliest map of The Crescent is that of the trustees of the Oxford Canal, dated 1828. No houses are shown, but comparing this with the 1837/8 Glebe map, which does show buildings, and checking land owned either side, whose ownership had not changed in the decade, it is possible to ascertain that a John Wilkinson owned and occupied the land. (No. 19 on the Canal map and its accompanying Terrier.) He does not appear to have owned or occupied land elsewhere in Brinklow, and as the canal map only refers to the land through which the canal passed when it was built around 1770, one cannot be sure that the house was built at that time. However, a date carved into a beam of a house of the same era in Post Office Yard, 1782, strongly suggests that it was, and that John Wilkinson lived in it.

The house may be even earlier; the cellar is certainly older than the house, so a previous house stood there. Also, a brick garage belonging to No. 11 at the bottom of the yard was originally on the far side of the canal, and is shown on the present deeds as one quarter of a much larger building, probably a warehouse. Equally, the Enclosure Award of 1742, although unfortunately not accompanied by a map, suggests that the yard was once a through road to the fields behind, access having been granted over the land of Matthew Colledge, who then owned it. The presence of a bridge (Watson's Bridge) on the canal map, which clearly shows a thoroughfare to land then known as Town Furlong, and to the later towpath, would seem to support this.

By at least 1837, the property was owned by a James Mason, who was a grocer and draper, and the Glebe map clearly shows the present building. The vast cellar, the full size of the property, and which also once included a small cellar in No.13, is far too large for an ordinary house. It is also well lit by a large window at the rear of the house, half above ground level, which was once barred, and was considerably larger than the other house windows; this would have been a surprising feature of a purely residential property of the era. Barred windows, especially ground floor ones are common from the early Georgian period; housebreaking and petty theft was as much, if not more of a problem then as it is now.

All this suggests that the property was built as a shop, probably serving customers from the back, (this was still happening within living memory), and probably provisioning boats on the canal. It appears feasible then, that John Wilkinson built the property, thinking that the canal would last for ever, and that business would boom, as it most probably did for a short time. He could scarcely have foreseen that Brinklow would lose its canal, trade would plummet, and someone would then have on their hands a very large house with an extraordinarily large cellar.

James Mason, a Brinklow man born and bred was still living in the property in June 1841, aged 35; he appears in the census for that year with his wife,

Elizabeth, sons John, James and Henry, and his daughter Jane. But by 1847, he had clearly given it up as a bad job, because in that year, a James Dunnicliffe, Grocer, was completing his land-tax return and his account of rents collected for Mrs. Elizabeth Mason, of London, using a small brown rent book, and lost them both down the back of a cupboard in the cellar of No. 11, not to be seen again for over a century.

Interestingly, the land tax return shows that the assessor who was responsible for the collection of dues also lived in Brinklow; in the 1841 census, the excise officer appears to live next door with his wife and family, although it is difficult to be certain of the enumerator's exact route. Later reports give No. 1 The Crescent as custom and excise officer's house.

The rents, which start off being collected quarterly, soon decline into an almost "get it when you can" system, some paying every three weeks, others weekly, at a variable rate of around 1s. 7d. per week. A landlord's lot was clearly not always an easy one; outgoings were considerable, including Land Tax, Poor Rate, Highway Rate, and Bailiff's expenses - evidently "moonlight flits" were also a problem, and the tenants seem to have changed very frequently. The rent book shows that not only had the property been divided up into two houses, but also that Mrs. Mason owned other property nearby, probably No. 15, and Long View, in Post Office Yard, then two, or possibly three cottages. In the 1851 census for Brinklow, not as a widow but a grocer's wife, she appears as a visitor further down the village. Although James Dunnicliffe appears in White's 1850 Directory for Brinklow as a grocer, he is not in the 1851 census, and the shop is now occupied by George D. Compton and his sister Marrianne, again as a grocer and draper. He was 22 and she was 29, keeping house for her brother and both unmarried; an oddly touching scenario. One can't help hoping things turned out well for them.

By 1861, however, another young couple, married this time, John and Annie Ayres had taken over, trading as grocers, chemists and druggists, and were still there in 1866, also acting as Postmaster. However, by the time of the 1871 census, Emily and Sophia Morris, spinster sisters from Higham on the Hill in Leicestershire had taken over, and the Post Office was no longer Emily's responsibility. In White's Directory for 1872, we find that it had moved down the road to Thomas Adler's.

In the 1881 census, the house and shop was uninhabited, or at least part of it was, because two elderly sisters, Elizabeth Beasley and Mary Mattocks, both from Leicestershire, appear to be living next door, and then appear in the property in 1891; in 1881 there seems to have been four households counting from the named "landmark" of Cleaver's Yard (later Post Office Yard) to the shop in the census, and not three as one would expect. The likely explanation is that in 1881, the sisters lived in the back of No. 11, and it was only the shop that was uninhabited. Both are "living on their own means" which probably means they were scraping a meagre living on their savings. The shop certainly didn't trade during those years, but it would appear that in 1887, the cellar was being lived in, because someone lost a ticket for Queen Victoria's Jubilee celebrations in Brinklow down the back of the cellar mantelpiece, again, not to be discovered for over a century.

The Directory for Warwickshire of 1896 clearly shows that the property had been taken over, renovated, and was set for purposeful business. The partnership of Brown & Bryan, Grocers, Tea-Dealers, & Provision

Merchants, selling tin, ironware, glass, brooms and brushes, was the start of a successful era for No. 11. George Brown was an old man who had been operating a small grocery business further down the village, and William Bartlett Bryan was his son in law, married to his daughter Annie. The partnership continued trading as Brinklow Supply Stores in 1900, becoming a Post Office again in 1906, when Brown either died or retired. At this time, the cellar was used as a sorting office, mail being dropped down a grating under the shop window.

Until 1928, a period of 32 years, Bryan ran the shop, and was obviously a pillar of the community, appearing on school committees and at social gatherings. He was succeeded by Charles James Bullock. By 1940, a character with the unlikely name of John Edward Nelson Fligg was Grocer and Postmaster, followed by people of the name of Moorehouse. A Mr. Matthews ran it for eight years in the 1960s, followed by Tom and Vera Moore, who retired and left the village in 1985. At that time, the Post Office moved to Broad Street, where it still is today. George and Diane Lindsay bought the house and empty shop premises in 1985, and in 1987 Brinklow Pottery opened, the cellar housing kilns and clay instead of wet fish, and the Royal Mail. The pottery closed in 2000 and is now a private house.

In approximately 200 years, No. 11, The Crescent has had 16 known owners or occupiers, and almost everything imaginable has been sold from the premises, from seed corn to knitting wool, from fish to a Penny Black, from patent medicines to flat-irons, from farthing chews to a haircut. From being one of, if not the earliest shop in the village on the canal, it became a specialist studio pottery with customers from every corner of the globe, and with the potter's mark of

"Brinklow", the name of the village is recorded from Paris to Peru. Visitors may notice the many ceramic house name plaques made in the Pottery.

It is in some ways strange to know the names, and something of the history of so many people who were here first, who have climbed the same stairs, looked out of the same bedroom window and seen the same moon sailing over the church, who have cursed when the rain comes straight down the same chimney, and who presumably crossed their fingers in much the same way every time it snows in case the roof gully needs sweeping out again.

We know a lot about them, but not yet enough. Who was it, for instance, who hid the beef bones and broken pitchers in between the floorboards, so that when the kitchen ceiling was being renovated, the whole astonishing lot crashed down with it? Whose oil lamp burned away most of a ceiling beam in the shop and was that the "big fire over the road", recorded in the school log-books that held up the schoolchildren and made them late nearly a hundred years ago? Who lost his collar studs, and who her penny purse down the back of the cellar mantel along with the Jubilee ticket? Who planted two earthenware ink bottles in the front shop foundations? And who, oh, who, put two large mummified frogs under the floorboards in the loft? If only the walls could talk!

Now known as Brinklow Supply Stores but still the Post Office Circa 1940

House History: Giles' Florist (Part Only)

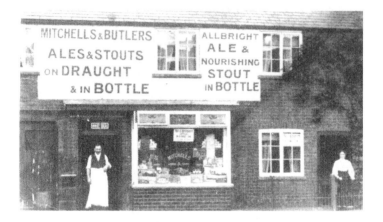

The Florists, now a private house, in an even earlier guise as an off licence.

The property in Broad Street which was the Florist's shop belonging to Rita and Graham Giles was, in 1771 the subject of an agreement between three parties, John Mieres, Honoria Holebeche and Mary Mieres, and one Thomas Neal to whom they sold the premises and land. There was a complex previous history of bequests which led to this tripartite ownership and thus the necessity for such an agreement; all of the vendors were required to give up all rights, including those of their heirs, in order to prevent future litigation from disgruntled descendants, who might otherwise claim that the property had not rightly been theirs to sell.

The story appears to be thus: in and before 1753, the property described as "extending from the common street westward to the late open and common fields of Brinklow" had been occupied, as tenants by John Smallbones, William Howard, Thomas Coaton, John Biber the Elder, and John Smith. The owner was Christopher Capel, "of the City of Coventry, gentleman..." who had bought it from John Pincher on 9th June 1753.

It was subsequently bequeathed to Christopher Capel's brother "and heir at law", John Capel, to "share and share alike." The relationship is not clear, but they may have been his nephews. James, however, went bankrupt, which meant that he could not inherit shared property, and Richard died in possession of it all, leaving it to his descendants, the Reverend John Mieres, of Coleshill, Honoria Holbeche (nee Mieres) and Mary Mieres, spinster, also of Coleshill. The actual agreement did not cite Honoria, the heiress alone, but also her husband, Amillian Holbeche, of the City of Lichfield, who by the law of the time, was entitled to "own" and administer his wife's property; married women, in law could not own anything of their own, as a wife was deemed to be her husband's property anyway. Mary, on the other hand, as a spinster, could own property until she married. The witness was Samuel Reader, Woolstapler, of Coventry.

The indenture is interesting, because not only does it date the property to at least 1753, it also shows that it may have been substantially older. It also reveals the names of local inhabitants in Brinklow at the time, and the common practice of absentee landlords collecting rents from property they probably never lived in. It is probable that the original sale came about due to Brinklow's Enclosures, from 1747, when by various private Acts of Parliament, common land was required to be enclosed and redistributed, and many smallholders' property ceased to be viable due to the crippling cost of legally enforced fencing. Most sold their small plots to bigger landowners, who thus acquired vast holdings which suited their new, more intensive arable farming policies. Poor cottagers, at this time were doubly penalised, as without the benefit of common grazing they could scarcely subsist, and many thus dispossessed rural families began to drift away to bigger towns and larger villages, for the first time seeking paid employment.

Thomas Neal purchased the property and its outbuildings and gardens in 1771 for the princely sum of "Thirty-eight pounds of lawful money of Great Britain. In 1896, Benjamin Tomlinson had the property and was using it as an off-licence, but ownership between and since has yet to be researched and documented.

From Common Land to Playing Field

It is interesting, and may be significant that the land which is now the playing field, once roughly the common ground, has again returned to communal use. This land was purchased in 1958 at a cost of £700, and this together with the additional cost of levelling, seeding and fencing, plus swings etc. was raised by grants, donations, a loan from the British Legion, and by every household in Brinklow contributing at least 1s. per week for four months. The moving spirits in this enterprise were Mrs. Violet Abbot, Mr. Ellis Tew, and Mr. John Brown.

Brinklow Mop

In the early 19th century, Brinklow held an annual Mop

Fair for the purposes of hiring labour amongst the surrounding community. People came from some distance according to local newspaper reports, which mostly seem concerned with catching out people trying to retain settlement. In order to gain settlement in a parish, which meant you and your family would be able to claim poor relief if in need, you needed to be born there, own land or prove you had worked there for a year and a day and ended that year with a full set of wages. Both employers and employees frequently tried to cheat this rule, in which case the issue went before a Board of Guardians, and if this didn't resolve the matter, a court of Petty Sessions. One of these was also held in Brinklow, often made up of the same local worthies in each case. A pauper found in breach would be summarily dismissed back to his or her place of birth so as to become a charge upon that parish. In 1823, it was reported in the Warwick and Warwickshire Advertiser that one William Gilbert hired at Brinklow Mop won his case against an employer who falsely stated he had paid his wages but he had not served his full year.

Pubs and Publicans in Brinklow

The Half Moon and Seven Stars circa 1900

As has already perhaps become obvious, Brinklow has always been well-supplied with alehouses. In this, it has been no different to any other community of a like size; the brewing and selling of ale has its roots in antiquity, and for centuries, workers have gathered in sociable groups after their labours over a jar. Originally, the Maltster, who supplied the malted grain for both beer and vinegar, was a high-status member of the community.

Not all of the present public houses are mentioned in the sources available for research, such as censuses, directories, etc. and we have no way of knowing if the alehouses which were suppressed in the 17th century are the same as the ones we patronise today. Almost certainly they were not, or if any were, they were probably informal places, someone's kitchen given over to the quaffing of home-brew of varying qualities.

The rural working man drank ale; it was all he could afford, and until the late 17th century, only cities were allowed to have taverns, where wine could be sold as well as beer and ale. The gentry and affluent middle classes drank at home, or more infrequently in larger coaching inns when roads became less dangerous and more conducive to travel. The late 18th century began the great coaching era, and consequently alehouses vied for the custom of travellers, offering where possible facilities for horses, and private sitting rooms where the better-off could refresh themselves away from the local rabble; many a lounge bar and snug have their origins in this segregation of the classes, and echoes of the practice still exist. Visitors to Brinklow are usually found in the superior decor (and higher prices) of the Lounge, whereas most locals prefer the spit-and-sawdust sociability of the Bar.

Two of the earliest known pubs in Brinklow seem to be The White Lion, and The Plough, now a private house in Broad Street, and still trading as a pub in 1850. A direct ancestor of many people still living locally was James Liggins, who possibly after an advantageous marriage to an Esther Glover, daughter of John Glover of Blaby, Gent, had an interest in both, and later in The Boat Inn, Easenhall.

The land upon which The White Lion stands was once known as Wale's Charity Lands, having been left to the Mayor and Aldermen of Coventry in 1624 by Thomas Wale on condition that they gave 40s per annum (a vast sum then) from the rents to the poor of Brinklow. Coventry Corporation then leased it to various persons, with conditions as to its upkeep, as a business proposition. These tenants then sublet, using the rents as income, a common practice.

In an Indenture (contract) of 1794 between the Mayor and Commonalty of Coventry and John Hodgins of Brinklow the previous tenants of the land and buildings upon it (named as "a ruinous cottage"), are Thomas Lichfield, David Cotton, Dorothy Marshall, Charles Morris, Bartholomew Howe, Thomas Heath and William Parnall. John Hodgins would seem to have acquired the lease in 1794, and this was renewed in 1811 for twenty-one years until 1832 on condition that he laid out £100 for erecting, building and maintaining "a good messuage (dwelling) and outbuildings", namely The White Lion Inn, by 1813. For this, £2 per annum was to be paid "before the Lord Mayor's Door in Cross Cheaping in the said City commonly called The Mayor's Walk". In the Indenture, which is extremely long and complex, the White Lion is named as being such in 1809, so probably "the ruinous cottage" was a drinking den long before the present superior building was erected.

In 1809, Jeremiah Jones was clearly the sub-tenant from John Hodgins, in association with Thomas Checkland and James Liggins; Jeremiah soon went bankrupt owing money to Thomas, and his goods and share were sold off to pay off his creditors; James Liggins was the best bidder, and so obtained a controlling share in the business, at a cost of £250. By 1818, he had sold his share to William Payne, who died in 1820, leaving it to Georgiana and Anne Payne. It then passed to John Brown (1821) who sold it to John Cryer in 1826.

In 1828 until at least 1837, the proprietor of the White Lion was William Cluley, but it doesn't seem to have given him a particularly good living, as after his death his wife, Ann was reduced to living in Rugby Workhouse. Subsequent proprietors were J. Hughes (1850-) Michael Spawton (1872-) who combined it with his business as a corn-dealer, T. Garret (1900-), Thomas Bartlett(1921-), Ernest Woodward (1936-) and William Lee (1940-) The present tenants are Ken and Mary Yeend.

Mr. Alan Turner, who now lives in Coventry, remembers a time, about 1918, when during summers he stayed at the White Lion for holidays, and as a boy encountered the cockerel "who liked his tipple". Apparently this Rhode Island Red, "high-stepping and red of face", would saunter down from the field beyond the bowling greens, stroll through the back door, up to the drip tray in the tap, and drink his fill. This happened every day about noon, and according to Mr. Turner, "no one interfered." Afterwards, he returned to the field, his step "faltering a bit," to give the hens "the sharp end of his beak."

Top: an early photograph of The White Lion. Mrs. West is standing in the doorway.

Below: Slightly later, showing the thatched cottages on the right and the big house, Sloan's Farm both of which were demolished.

Top: The Raven Inn with the Dean family circa 1913

Below: The Bull's Head on the left and The Dun Cow
on the right circa 1930

Both The Dun Cow and The Bull's Head are mentioned in the 1837 Glebe Terrier as properties obliged to pay tithes for the upkeep of the rector and for Poor Relief, in common with all other owner occupiers in Brinklow. Proprietors of the Dun Cow were: Thomas Curtis (1837-) Edward Barker (1872/1880)who also acted as a cattle dealer, Thomas Smith (1896-) W. H. Yates (1900-) and Herbert English (1936-).

Proprietors of The Bull's Head were Thomas Thompson (1837-), Thomas Haswell (1866-), Joseph Haynes (1871-),William Rowe, who combined it with horse breaking (1880-) Isaac Boyes (1921-) Oscar Varnish (1925-) and Frank Hammond (1936-). In 1900, the Oddfellows, a friendly society into which everyone paid a small sum, and received financial help in times of sickness, met every month in The Bull's Head. Mr. Bill Smith also remembers the "Hanging Jacks" performing there in the early 1920s, hard men from the canals and roads who earned the price of a pint by allowing themselves to be chained and hung upside down to see how quickly they could get free. In the 1930s and 40s, another "sick club" flourished for a while in The Bull's Head, and many people will remember the "sick visitor" who made sure no one claimed fraudulently; woe betide anyone "on the sick" who was seen out after 9 o'clock at night.

The Raven Inn

The earliest mention of **The Raven Inn** directly is surprisingly only in 1850; it merits no mention in the census before 1880, but the building is plainly older than that. It is still a comparatively small pub, so perhaps it was a pub of the "alehouse kitchen" type, and never a coaching inn. Not every proprietor paid to be featured in directories, so absence from these isn't necessarily significant, but absence from the early censuses is puzzling. The building was clearly there, and someone was living in it, but without a name or a known landmark, it is difficult to establish who that person was. However the first known proprietors do seem to be John and Hannah Hayes, established from the Glebe terrier and map. Certainly their son, John appears in the 1841 census in the same place as a publican so this does seem to confirm that finding. In 1850, it was being run by a T. Glenn, followed by Miss Hannah Buggins (1866-) but who appears to own the land in the 1837 Glebe Terrier) Thomas Shepherd (1871-), Ellen Bird (1891) Mrs. Ellen Seymour (1896-), W. Smith (1900) William N. Smith (1901) Reuben Dean (1914) Frank Griffin (1921-), G. Goggerty (1924-), and Rudolph Bartlett (1936-). In 1900, The Female Friendly Society met in The Raven Inn once a month.

In 1837, The Half Moon and Seven Stars was owned by Sir Grey Skipworth, but was run by George Blundell. At various times in its career, it doubled as a Post Office, an informal magistrate's court, and an office for the local registrar. At one time, there appears to have been a slaughterhouse behind it. Subsequent proprietors were Jonathan Mullis (1866-) Edward Beamish (1880-) George Templeman (1896-) W. West (1900-) Frederick Cox (1921-) Mrs. Cox (1927-) and Charles Scampton (1936-).

In 1830, the Beerhouse Act made it legal for any householder to sell beer from his or her own home, on payment of two guineas, and so we can be fairly certain that Brinklow had an abundance of beersellers. In 1866, Richard Adkins is listed as a grocer and Beer Seller, in 1861 and 1871, Thomas Wolfe managed to reconcile his duties as Methodist Lay Preacher with that of Beer

Seller and agent for Insurance, a Liberal Club once stood next to South View, and the Institute Building at the bottom of Broad Street once housed a Conservative Club, and later a Working Man's Club. In the Institute, dinners, dances, concerts and other club meetings were a regular feature of village life; one elderly resident remembers that the road outside was strewn with straw before a dance, to muffle the noise of horses' hooves, which suggests that visitors came then, as now, from far and wide to enjoy Brinklow's social life.

The Royal British Legion

The Brinklow Branch of the Royal British Legion was formed in 1951 at a meeting in the Church rooms, when everyone present contributed 2s. 6d. Early meetings were held in the White Lion, until 1963, when a shop and living accommodation was purchased in Heath Lane, and converted to a Headquarters and social club, largely by members themselves. The branch itself is a registered charity, and by law the accounts of the social club and branch have to be kept separate. The charity exists mainly for the welfare of ex-servicemen and women and their dependants, and as during the second war almost every family in Brinklow had someone in uniform, the British Legion is very much part of Brinklow's life.

In 1953, the branch started giving Christmas gifts to pensioners in the village, originally of two bags of logs each, then added a parcel of groceries, and now a monetary gift. In the beginning, there were 50 people on the list; in 1993, there were approximately 200. (Married couples count as one.)

In 1952, the Legion started the Annual Remembrance Sunday Church Parade, and they are also responsible for reinstating Brinklow's traditional Wake Sunday Parade and service.

Leisure time in Brinklow

It seems that Brinklow people have always worked hard and played hard. Although many older residents recall the hard times, and there were many, the most delightful memories are often those in which the villagers let down their hair and enjoyed themselves. In her diary, Mrs. Friswell records Morris dancers in the streets on Plough Monday, January 9th 1882, on July 10th, the Oddfellows Anniversary Procession, on the 11th, The Women's Club Procession, Sports held on the hill on 15th July, and the School's Annual Tea-Drinking on August 4th.

Winter was frequently enlivened with ice-skating expeditions, both on the canal and at Newbold Revel, and for a fortunate few, Grand Balls at Coombe Abbey. The Rugby Advertiser has many accounts of concerts, magic lantern shows, and dances in the village, there were the various School and Sunday Schools' treats and outings, and the occasional organised excursion by train.

On May 1st, there was dancing around a maypole erected on the green, and a May Queen was chosen, and then, as now, throughout the year there were Fetes, Sales of Work, Bazaars and copious "tea-drinking" (which seems to be an early form of the "coffee morning") to raise funds for various good causes Although self-contained, Brinklow does not ever seem to have been an insular village, with every opportunity being taken for socialising with other nearby villages, and always a number of sociably minded residents prepared to organise events and raise money for good causes. If this last could be linked to the whole village enjoying a holiday, or an outing, or just rubbing shoulders, so much the better.

The Church Rooms in Brinklow were donated by Dr. Hair in memory of his son, Donald, who was killed in the early years of World War I.

BRINKLOW WAKE.

ON MONDAY NEXT, July 12th, an EXCUR-SION BY WATER from COVENTRY to BRINKLOW and COMBE ABBEY, will take place, it being Brinklow Wake, when a Boat or Boats will proceed from Coventry Canal Wharf, near the Toll Gate, calling at all the Bridges between there and Brinklow. Arrangements have been made to enable parties to view the Celebrated ABBEY & GROUNDS at COMBE.

Quadrilles and Country Dances, Cricket and Foot Ball, Quoits, Walking, Running, Leaping, Archery, Drop Handkerchief, Kissing in the Ring, and other Exercises.

Fares, and Time of Starting and Departure:—
Leaves Coventry at 7½, arr. at Brinklow at 12 6d. each.
" Foleshill Bridges from 8 to Half-past 5d. "
" Longford Wharf at 9 .... 4½d. "
" Stop and Tusses' Bridge at 9½ .... 4d. "
" Anstey at 10 .... 3d. "
Returning from Brinklow at 5½ and arriving at Coventry at 9 p.m. Children Threepence each.

Parties returning from Brinklow who do not go with the Boat, must pay the above Charges in full.

For the accommodation of parties who do not wish to take their own Provisions, REFRESHMENTS will be provided on Board at Cost Price. Tea at Brinklow at 4 o'clock at 6d. each.

N.B. All parties must provide the amount of their Fare before going on Board, as no Change will be given them. Tickets to be had of Mr. CHARLES SATCHELL, Coventry, and Mr. T. BURDETT, Longford, on or before Saturday next, July 10th.

Coventry Times Wednesday 7ᵗʰ July 1858

BRINKLOW.

THE RAVEN INN,

A. J. LISSAMAN .... Proprietor.

Choice Wines and Spirits, Finest Ales and Stouts on Draught, every accommodation for Cyclists. Dinners and Teas provided. Cigars of the Choicest Brands. Pony and trap on hire. A nice walk up the Flower Garden on to the Brinklow Hills.

MRS. WEST,

WHITE HOUSE, BRINKLOW.

Teas provided for Small Parties, with use of Brinklow High Hills. Parties wishing to visit these hills, apply to the above. No other person can give permission.

Coventry Evening Telegraph 14th June 1899

Known as the "Hanging Jacks" men, usually from the canal boats would allow themselves to be hung upside down outside the pubs and betting would take place as to how long it would take them to escape from their chains and ropes. A portion of the pot would go to buy their drinks that day.

Crook House: Once, the candle master John How's house, then a tea rooms with stables and cycles for hire, now a private home.

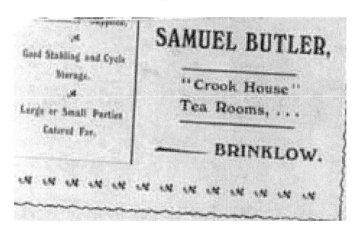

SAMUEL BUTLER,

Good Stabling and Cycle Storage.

"Crook House" Tea Rooms, . . .

Large or Small Parties Catered For.

BRINKLOW.

Lewins' shop: now the hairdressers Carole Elizabeth

*The Curiosity Shop now Brinklow House Chinese
takeaway and Chip shop*

Ernie Johnson and Toby. Behind him is The Manse,
now the Post Office and Pumpkin Deli

Broad Street Circa 1940 when it was still called Main Street. Who remembers Thorley's Old Peculiar?

An Exile Remembers

For a period between 1853 and 1861, Charles Samuel Compton, born in 1821 at Harborough Fields Farm was the baker in Brinklow. Charles Samuel married Sarah Hinde Rose at Hatton in 1845, after a life roving the high seas and exploring the New World with his brother Robert. He had many adventures, and when he finally came home and settled down, he took up his old profession, the one he had been apprenticed to as a boy, in order to feed his growing family; the bakery was in Broad Street, where the Adnitt family lived until recently.

Sadly, in 1861, a baby, Louisa was born, and died, and Sarah died two days later, both being buried in Brinklow churchyard. Charles was left a widower with five children aged between 13 and 2, and in the face of this tragedy, it wasn't long before he took the decision to emigrate. In 1863, he left for Canada, taking Charles,4, Edward, 7, Mary Jane, 11, and Maria Louisa Jackson, a young woman engaged to look after the children. His two eldest, Elizabeth 15, and Harry, 13, stayed behind, Harry joining them in Kingston, Ontario in 1865.

Charles Samuel found happiness in his new country; in 1866, he married the nursemaid, and had four more children by her. His son, William Henry (Harry,) however, never forgot Brinklow where he had plainly spent a happy youth, and is thought to have returned several times for visits. His sister, Elizabeth, never went to Canada, but kept up a close correspondence with her far away family.

Charles Samuel had an elder brother, William, from whom descended another William Henry Compton, and his son Mr. Robert Compton, cattle dealer, late of Brinklow. Robert Compton's son, another Robert, emigrated himself some years ago, but his daughter, Miss Leonora Compton still lives in the village. Harry wrote the following letter just after World War I, from Kingston to his first cousin William Henry in Brinklow, and a copy was sent to Brinklow History group by Charles Samuel's great granddaughter Marjorie Simmons who still lives in Kingston, Ontario, is a long distance member of the History Group, and has given permission to use the fruits of her research into her Brinklow roots:

450 Frontenc St. Kingston, Ontario. Sept 2nd Mr. William Henry Compton, Brinklow.

Dear Kinsman,

Although a thousand leagues separate us, that is no reason we should forget we are first cousins, and that we once met at your father's dying bed at Leamington in or about the year 1877. Your brother Charley came to visit me at Toronto, when he came with Aunt Bateman to visit my dear old father, who has passed onto the land of the spirits, and I his eldest son miss him more than one can tell. I also look back to the dear old Harborough Fields, the ancestral home, with feelings of sorrow, now that it has passed out of the Compton family, as I spent many happy days with my dear old Uncle Tom and Aunt Sophia, when I used to herd swine and sheep, and do all that a boy could do, not out of nursing strings: indeed, it was there that I first learned of the death of my dear mother, whose mortal body lies sleeping in your village churchyard, where I have never visited since I wept tears as I saw her dear form lowered into the grave.

Yes, cousin, I often wonder if Tom Ashmore, the painter, is still living in the village, as he helped to bear her body, as did Mr. Dalton, the baker, and Mr. Sidwell, the schoolmaster, who was my very dear friend, as well as my mother and father. I suppose it is unlikely that any of the old folk I mention are now living, yet ages seem to have been prolonged of late, and I know an old lady who has passed her century mark, and some are much older; and should there be any living who knew me as a boy, give my best regards and tell them I would love to get a letter as I pass most of my time writing, and if Polly is living, give her my kindest regards and to your family, all remember me kindly, as I think that kinsmen of so old a family as ours ought never to let earthly vanities separate or estrange for if we do not live friendly here upon earth, we are not likely to be comfortable if perchance we were to get into heaven. Finally, if you wish to hear more concerning our family over here, write me about yours and what yours are doing; and if your brother Charley was killed in last war as reported in our papers. By the way my son Marcus was all through that war, shot thrice, gassed once, and although near done up, was miraculously spared and is now clerking in the Marine stores at Montreal.

P.S. Since writing the foregoing I have been taken to our hospital and operated for hernia, and I am home again feeling much better; hence in my absence the letter was not posted owing to the uncertainty of life, but God be thanked for the privelage of finishing some *necessary work; and I hope someday to publish my little book of father's voyages , as also my own wanderings; and should I do so, I will send you a book; but until my finances improve, it must remain like many another good intent "in esse futuro". The lackey bullies of Canada are so deplorably wicked that it is doubtful if the monsters do not provoke another war soon which must set the earth afire and cannibalize the universe. But God be with you all is the prayer of your affectionate kinsman**

William Henry Compton

Sarah Hinde Rose and Charles Samuel Compton

Law and Order in the 17th century

(Extracted from the records of the National Archives and Warwick Quarter Sessions)

Life for ordinary people in the 17th century was much more restricted than we are used to today; in 1601, the care of the poor was placed, by law, in the care of each individual parish, and those who fell upon hard times, such as illness, infirmity or old age were legally entitled to apply to their parish for help. A person was recognised as being a legally settled inhabitant of a parish after one month's abode, and although this was later increased to forty days, parish vestries soon began to operate an unofficial system of refusing relief to paupers who they could prove had settlement in another parish. As the money for relief was raised by tithes, and the parish authorities were often people who had no real idea of how life was for labouring families, injustices often occurred. There was no recourse for those in distress but to take their plea to court for arbitration; this was very much the end of the line, and pleas were only usually brought as a last resort:

In 1649, Hugh Davenport of Brincklowe petitioned the court to order the parish authorities to house him, his wife and three small children, after a Mr. Clark had evicted them. Davenport had "sustained great loss by the soldiers in these late wars" (the Civil war), and had clearly been wounded to the point where he could not work or pay his rent. The court ruled that he and his family were "likely to perish unless speedy cause be taken to their relief", and ordered the constable, churchwardens and overseers of the poor to remedy the situation forthwith, as Davenport had successfully shown that he had been resident in Brinklow for the past ten years.

Sometimes landlords took the law into their own hands; the Quarter Sessions papers are full of instances of the weak and vulnerable being dealt summary justice by those with no authority:

In 1639, Elizabeth Bentham, widow, was "forcibly ejected" from her house by William and Ann Dawes, their son, and his friend the local baker. The court fined them, but it isn't clear whether Mrs. Bentham got her home back. The law concerning trades often worked against anyone trying to supplement their income, or expand an existing business:

In 1682, William Geases of Brincklow, labourer, was fined for using the trade of grocer for seven months "contrary to the statute". John Mason, tailor, was also fined on the same occasion for "using the trade of mercer for the like time".

Even in the 17th century, Neighbourhood Watch was called for. In 1684, John Adkins, labourer, Samuel Pace, husbandman, Samuel Smith, yoeman, Edward Sale the younger, husbandman, all of Brincklowe and Thomas Bird of Long Lawford were sent to the Assizes (a higher court) for "...breaking into the dwelling of one Henry Dann of Brincklowe and feloniously taking away of certain goods out of the same house".

Unbelievably harsh treatment was meted out for immorality, but women's rights had a very long way to go in the 17th century; sometimes pregnant women were driven outside the parish boundary to avoid the claim that the offspring had a right to settlement and thus be a financial drain on the community.

In 1864, Kathleen Dudley of Brincklowe was "committed to the House of Correction for bastardy, there to remain by the space of one whole year and to be set to hard labour". Afterwards ordered to be whipped and discharged.

George Parnell was *"to allow weekly towards the maintenance of a male bastard child begotten by him on the body of the said Kathleen"*.

The authorities disapproved of informal arrangements between parents and employers, given that this was often tantamount to selling one's child into slavery for seven years; a legal apprenticeship, (which might in fact be no kinder on the apprentice,) was usually paid for by parent or guardian. In the case of orphans, the parish paid the indenture fee, hence orphans often had a very hard time indeed, often beaten, starved and abused, with no one to speak for them. Given that apprenticeships could begin as young as eight in the 17th century, one wonders why the following plea was brought; sadly the reasons for it don't seem to have merited recording:

In 1698, on information on behalf of George Johnson the younger, apprentice to Robert Habbert of Monk's Kirby, butcher, that his master "has no business to employ him" the court ordered his father, George Johnson the Elder to place him instead with Edward Dickens of Brincklowe to serve out his time.

Often, parishes would dispute hotly whether those seeking poor relief were their responsibility, and wherever possible, would unload paupers onto another parish, thus saving money; this led to the terrible spectacle of the poor, aged or infirm being driven considerable distances, sometimes to places where they knew no one or might be far worse off.

In 1691, Richard Riley and Ann, his wife, "poor people" were ordered to be removed to Catesby in Northamptonshire, despite swearing under oath that they were settled at Brinklow Later, the Settlement laws were altered, and in 1795, removal by the Overseers of the Poor was forbidden unless the pauper actually became a charge upon the parish, and this did away with some of the injustices, although the principle of settlement remained in force until 1876. Astonishingly, it was only removed from the statute book in 1948.

Parochial "convenient houses of dwelling for the impotent poor" were set up in 1601, but workhouses only became widespread in the 18th century. In 1834, Poor Law Unions took over responsibility for the poor from the parish, and were usually in the nearest town; Brinklow paupers would have been sent to Rugby. Often in age, people who could no longer work, and whose families were themselves so hard pressed they couldn't afford to keep them, ended their days in these dreary places; couples who had lived together most of their lives were separated, and children housed apart from their parents. For the mentally ill, or the confused, people suffering from epilepsy, or even young women who became pregnant and were deemed criminally immoral were often transferred from the workhouse to the lunatic asylum.

Although undoubtedly many Brinklow residents ended their days in these grim institutions, the censuses of the 19th century show many instances of families caring for their aged and infirm; the horror of the workhouse perhaps goes a long way towards explaining why parents were prepared to let even very small children work extraordinarily long hours, and why we find old men of 80 still giving their occupation as "labourer".

The Brinklow Association for the Prosecution of Felons

In the 18th and early 19th centuries, before the creation of a national police force, rural communities formed mutual subscription societies to prosecute criminals. These evolved out of resolutions passed at parish vestry meetings to prosecute felons out of the public purse. Printed handbills declaring the intentions of such bodies and offering rewards for information leading to an arrest are sometimes found in local record offices, and notices of the activities of such associations are reported in local newspapers. Brinklow formed its own Association for the Prosecution of Felons and documents held in the National Archives tell of one such prosecution in March 1791.

Two petitions were heard before at the Warwickshire Assizes on 19 March 1791 before a judge and twenty four people, including members of the Brinklow Association for the Prosecution of Felons, a teacher from Rugby School, an attorney at law, an ensign in the 43rd regiment and a captain of the Warwickshire Militia on behalf of Edward Harris, and William Terry, millers, convicted (with George Beeby who was eventually reprieved). The charge was burglary and stealing a till containing some guineas and an amount of silver and other goods, from the shop of John House, at Brinklow, on the night of 26/27 November 1790. This is almost certainly John Howe, rather than House and would have been in and around where Crook House and Tallow Cottage is today in the Crescent, behind which was the Candle Factory.

The petition contains full details of the house and its construction and 'the most convenient place' for the house to be broken into. Edward Harris came from Rugby while William Terry was from Banbury in Oxfordshire. An accomplice, John Kench, had turned King's evidence; and John Barratt, another accomplice, was still at large. Ann Lines was indicted for receiving goods from the burglary but not convicted.

The judge considered Harris to have been part of a gang that had caused great trouble in the area and Terry the 'most active offender.' The information of the accomplice accused Terry of five instances of housebreaking and a sixth of highway robbery. Magistrates had also informed the judge that Harris was 'the terror of that neighbourhood.' Grounds for clemency were considered, including the youth of the accused (Harris was 26 and Terry only 19) that they had fallen in with bad company, their good behaviour during confinement, and that they were truly repentant, asking for commutation of their sentence to transportation for life. Mercy, it was suggested would alleviate the distressed feelings of family and friends; and that Harris was from a respectable Rugby family. The sentence was death with no recommendation: no mercy.

RUGBY UNION.

CLERK, Mr. G. V. HERFORD, Rugby.

ONATHAN HAYES, labourer, aged 41: height 5-ft 7½-in. brown hair and whiskers, hazel eyes, and sallow complexion; has a very erect military walk; has served in the Army about 9 years, and was discharged in 1849; had on when he left home a fustian jacket with outside pockets and sporting buttons, a dark mixed cloth waistcoat, corduroy trousers, a pair of light Wellington boots with high heels, and a dark-brown or black billy-cock hat; and is ship-tatooed on the right arm. Deserted his wife and seven children about two months ago, leaving them chargeable to the Parish of Brinklow, in the Rugby Union.

One Pound Reward will be paid to any one who will apprehend him.

This extract from the Poor Law Union Gazette of 1861 shows that a wanted man wasn't always necessarily a felon.

Trades and Professions

Tree fellers actively involved in felling the tall elms that once stood on the Tump

Agriculture and rural trades were long the main source of employment for Brinklow people, although a slow but increasing decline is evident from the early censuses to the last available one in 1911. Most of those employed were labourers, whose work was often seasonal, and in many of the censuses, the chilling words "out of employ" occur again and again. The major employers were Coombe Abbey, Town Thorns and to a lesser extent Newbold Revel and Newnham Paddox. In 1861, nine residents gave their occupation as "farmer", with two more "out of business"; this had declined in 1891 to seven, plus one "retired". These would have been land owners or more often tenant farmers, employing some men and boys. Associated occupations found in the censuses are ploughboy, (eleven in 1871, none in 1891), grazier, carter, waggoner, shepherd, and gardener (ten in 1871, and in 1891). By the 1911 census, many people were able to travel out of Brinklow to surrounding towns for employment and occupations reflect this.

The majority of women went into some form of service; again the major employers being the great houses until their eventual decline. Most describe themselves as "general servant", but others are more specific, with housemaid, housekeeper, cook, laundress and "charwoman", (seven in 1871, none in 1891). With the opening of the Silk Mill, many women were engaged as silk throwsters, winders, trimming makers and "glimp makers" (another form of trimming). However, fashion, together with the removal of the import duty on foreign ribbons gradually reduced this kind of work, and in 1891, fourteen women were outworking as stay makers.

Other male occupations were groom, footman, coachman; the coming of the railways, the improvement of the roads and the canal at Stretton Wharf provided more opportunities for work, although even there it is obvious that a general drift to the towns was taking place. In 1861, there were five blacksmiths in Brinklow, but in 1891, only two, Mr. Wilkins and Mr. Edwards; in 1871, there were ten brick-makers, and in 1891, none, although there were still six brick-layers as opposed to eleven in 1871.

Cordwainers or shoemakers were strongly represented, with nine in 1861, and six still in operation in 1891; the Manger family in Crook House Yard and Mr. Perkins near the White Lion are remembered in

Miss Cryer's notes. Miss May Bayliss and her family were noted for their basket-making, and had their own osier beds in Heath Lane, where there was also a corn mill. Miss Fitter, midwife and nurse lived at Friswell's Farm.

Many people went into trade in a larger or smaller way. Every census contains a far larger number of butchers, bakers, and grocers than we would expect the village to support today, and with corn merchants, seed merchants, feed merchants, horse dealers, cattle dealers, plumbers and coalmen, straw hat makers, even in 1891, an "Old Curiosity Dealer", the Brinklow of the past must have been virtually self-sufficient.

Even if the settlement that Brynca's people founded only occasionally flirted with prosperity, and if, like the canal the candle factory, and the silk mill and the almost-built branch line of the railway, Brinklow never got the moment quite right, we, Brynca's newest people have to thank our stoical, dogged, gritty, determined, argumentative, bawdy, feckless and even rascally predecessors, for the finest legacy of all. For surviving; for never allowing Brynca's Low to sleep under the green turf of a Warwickshire meadow, like Smite, and Hopsford, and so many that went before, for handing us, in trust for those who come tomorrow, a living village.

Once a slaughterhouse, The Shambles, then Walkers Butchers, now a private dwelling; 14th century pottery shards were discovered here.

Looking down Broad Street. Inset is the Church Hall and beyond that is the shop that was Stengers. The thatched cottage was demolished after a firework set fire to the thatch.

Below: The junction of Coventry Road and Broad Street. The big house on the left is the Sloan's Farm which is seen at the bottom of Broad Street in the picture above. Beyond it is The Larches looking towards Heath Lane

ELIAS HOWE: BRINKLOW'S LEAST KNOWN FAMOUS 4X GRANDSON

Elias Howe Jr 1819-1867 is thought to be the four times great grandson of one John Howe, who arrived in the Massachusets Bay Colony in America in 1630 from Brinklow. This first John Howe was apparently the first white man to settle in the town of Marlborough, and also went on to help found another town, Sudbury. One of his sons, David owned The Wayside Inn, where Longfellow spent much of time writing his famous poems.

Elias was the inventive son of Dr. Elias Howe, and as a young man was apprenticed to a firm of precision instrument manufacturers. Whilst there he developed and refined earlier concepts of a sewing machine and patented the first machine using lockstitches, with a needle with an eye at the point, a shuttle and an automatic feed.

He had considerable trouble finding backers however both in America and in England but eventually was successful in winning royalties from Isaac Singer who had copied his patent. Elias's patent won the gold medal at the 1867 Paris Exhibition and he was awarded the *Legion d'honneur* by Napoleon III for his invention.

Both Elias Howe and Isaac Singer became multi-millionaires, and the Beatles 1965 film Help is dedicated to Howe in its closing credits.

AND ONE OF BRINKLOW'S SADDEST DAUGHTERS:

BRINKLOW

An inquest was held on Monday last, the 19th inst., at the Half Moon and Seven Stars, [Brinklow] before W. H. Seymour, Esq., Coroner, on the body of Sarah Walton, a schoolmistress in [Brinklow] It appeared from the evidence that she purchased two-pennyworth of arsenic, in the presence of a Mrs. Bottrill, and the shopman wrote upon the paper "Poison," and advised her to be careful in the use of it. She took it in the course of the following day, and shortly after died. Francis Oldacre, surgeon, had opened the body, and found the inner coat of the stomach much corroded, as would be the case from an irritating poison; the stomach was three parts full of food, chiefly undigested, and the appearance of the stomach was such as would be produced by arsenic, and he had no doubt she died from this poison; she was between 60 and 70 years of age, and a single woman. Verdict—"Destroyed herself while in a state of temporary insanity."

Early Place and Field Names,
including Coombe and
Coombefields (Smite)

It's very difficult, without a very early map to work out where these places were. I have kept the spelling of the originals plus the lack of apostrophes and grammar. Many field and place names go back so far that sometimes the original relevance is lost. Some are named for people who held the land at one time or another, and others sound strange to our ears because they are strong dialect words or over time have been corrupted into something else. After the enclosure of the three big fields of Brinklow, Ell, Brook, and Licence, where tenants formerly had strips of land in several places, smaller fields or closes were created. It was more economic but not always good for small farmers who sometimes received less fertile land or could not afford the legal upkeep of fences and so sold out to the bigger landowners. Another large field, Wood, was almost certainly land going up Wood Hill out of the village towards Coombe.

Generic terms, like field, land, ley, combe, close, croft, meadow, grove, gap, ground, piece and furlong are standard in meaning which I have explained in the tables. Others are descriptive of crops or local landmarks like trees etc. that could have disappeared long before. All bear a strong relationship to agriculture.

Many of the field and place names on the 1838 Glebe map seem to have a much earlier origin, and often provide evidence for which there is no other source. Some recall an industry or activity that once took place on the site; Brick Kiln names recall a brickmaking industry which was already clearly established by 1837, Butt Furlong, Great and Little Bowman's Meadows probably hark back to the days when every village had to be capable of providing trained bowmen if called upon by their feudal lord. Dove House Close was perhaps the site of a medieval dovecote, maintained not for pleasure, but as an extra supply of food for castle or manor, Hawkers Leys may be where the lord's retainers trained his sporting hawks, Monk's Riding, Priest's Bridge and Lane speak for themselves and echo the village's connections with Coombe Abbey. Other old field names refer to the fertility or otherwise of the area, and to the usual crop; thus we have many Clover, Rye , Furze, Pease, Orchard and Sun names, and none of the Hungry, Lean or Starveling type of names, which often found elsewhere, denote poor ground. Brinklow, as any gardener will agree, is even now an extraordinarily fertile place.

Other names hark back to the open field system of the Anglo-Saxon period, when most settlements had only two or sometimes later three large fields divided into strips. A bundle of strips running in one direction was known as a furlong, an element in many of Brinklow's field names - significantly mostly around the oldest part of the village towards Smeaton Lane. On a day of strong sunlight and shadow, Brinklow's ancient strip system is clearly visible, and the three field pattern clearly discernible in the larger parish map. Field name study is an area of research in itself, and within the scope of a general history such as this, can only be touched upon. Suffice it to say, Brinklow's field names reflect a fertile, sheltered and well-watered and ancient settlement.

Originally, before the economic demands of 18th century developments in farming methods led to a complete distribution of land, and the enclosure of the fields thus formed through various private Enclosure Acts, every villager would have had his (or occasionally her) own strips to cultivate, including a reasonably fair distribution of good and poor soils. Ploughing and harvesting was a communal affair, but clearly more conscientious villagers suffered from the weeds of their more feckless neighbours. However, each villager had the right to graze livestock on the common land or waste, (which appears to have been behind Broad Street, roughly where the playing fields are now) and also to collect firewood from it, which enabled even the very humble to maintain a reasonable level of subsistence. With Enclosure, and its consequent legal obligations to provide and maintain expensive fences and hedges, many of the smaller subsistence farmers began to sell off their small fields to the larger landowners, and drift to the new, sprawling industrial towns and villages. Thus, many families who today have no connection with the land, have their origins rooted in the soil of these dispossessed "yeomen" of England.

Bray's Close, Colledge Close, Skipwith Close and Brierley's Farm all owe their names to large landowning families past and present, while Potter's Close may recall the site of some early kilnworks. Great Balance is an early field name, Hall Grove was named after Lady Hall, who formally opened it, and Cathiron Lane seems to be, obscurely, a corruption of Catherine. Other local place names have yet to be researched, some presenting something of a problem. Barr Lane for instance, appears to be ancient, yet it has in more recent times been known as Park Lane. As yet, no clue to the origin of Crook House and the adjacent yard has come to light, although it may have been built on the site of a former "cruck" house. Broad Street was earlier known as Main Street, although it isn't clear when the change came about. An interesting example of modern name-forming is Fog Cottages, in Smeaton Lane, so called because originally, they belonged to the railway, and on receiving a fog warning, workmen had to go ahead to lay fog "caps" on the line, which when the train crossed over them, made a great bang, thus warning the engine driver of fog ahead.

For further information on and extracted lists of local place names, see Appendices I, II and III.

APPENDIX I
PLACE NAMES TAKEN FROM DOCUMENTS HELD IN THE SHAKESPEARE BIRTHPLACE TRUST ARCHIVES, STRATFORD UPON AVON

Year	Reference	Comments
1150	The Church of the Blessed Mary of Coombe	Coombe Abbey: Roger de Mowbray gifted Brinklow to the monks of Coombe for eighty marks in Frankalmoign (freee alms). That is he let them off military duties for a sum of money and their prayers for his souls
1161	..that part of his (Roger de Mowbray) wood of Brincalawa called Burthleia from Walwwei to Brandonie and Bilenie	Remember that the ways to Brandon and Binley would be in the forest of Arden, heavily wooded with assarts (clearings). Walewei may refer to Tutbury lane, an old paved trackway. Burhtleia is Birchley. It also refers to Maiweia which may mean Moor way
1240	La Wodegrange	Wood Grange. Granges were outlying estates in monastic ownership and their management was different and more efficient to village fields and strip farming.

1300 - 1312	Hamo Underwode of Brandaune had land in Brinklow	Great Baneland, Le Crosfurlong, Le Inheth (heath- Heath Lane?) Muckle Baneland, le Yondre Barre, (Barr Lane?) although in Celtic barre means hilltop) Fosse Furlong next the land of the Church, Super Castellum next Neubold Mor, le wode dych, Ruycroft, le Pedelar Brigge, Hotehulle next Redlond, Barr Dych.
1326	Gift from Henry Colemon to his daughter Agnes and Henry le Cartere in free marriage	Hondingwonge (land on a slope) le Stoniceche (stone church)
1335- 1336- 1345	Gift from Gilbert Edward to his daughter Agnes	Sur le Rocus Nestus – (Rooks Nest) Peshull (Peasehill) Sowemer (Sowe Mer -Sowe flood plain) Colmercroft.
1345		A certain piece of meadow named Smedole in the common meadows of Brynkelpwe below the Abbey of Cuma (Coombefields) dole suggests share or portion. This could be Smite as old

		pronunciation was Smeet as in Smee Town. (The town of the Smith in Old English)
1348 - 1369	William Blacsole	Ochull –Oakhill; Bonere - Bow Mere; Wodewell - Wood Well; Nunnewonge – Nun's Land; Wodegrene - Wood Green; Esenhull- Easenhall; attelyttole Brygge - at the little bridge; le Tounfurlong - Town Furlong; Heye Pessul; High Peas Hill; le Mulnacris - Mill Acres.
1369/ 70	Henry Coleman - Chaplain	The field of Nethergrene at Prustebrigge (Priest Bridge) between the water course towards the pool and a piece of land called Crosfurlong, which piece of meadow is called luttelprestes bruggebhok
1473		Warnerscrofte- Warner's Croft; Ankeriding - grassy pasture; le Kingespiece; Yuch Hell-Henchman's Hole, dwelling of a henchman or retainer; Sondepittes- Sand Pits; Ottehull-Otter Hill, At the Hill; Wyne yards- Vineyards
1474		Tutburywey –Tutbury Way
1477/8		Clayyarde -Clay yard

		(Brick Kiln?)
1496/7		Parknsyardforlong- Perkins Yard Furlong. Yardland was usually about 30 acres and villeins who had such a holding were eligible for reeveship or beadles office.
1497/8		Innychforlong – ench (hench as in henchman's furlong; Le Coomenbalk - common balk; boundary, not necessary unenclosed or uncultivated
1588		Castell Hills – Castle Hills (by 1588, the earthworks would be overgrown and seen as hills)
1626		Castell Hills in Brincklow, the moat around the same and fishing rights
1637		The Milnyard – Mill Yard; Costans Hook…the Hook Close – cost means cottager and hoc means corner of land in this instance. Hill Close; Orchard Close;Town Close; Hell Meadowe -Hill Meadow; Crabtree Close; Crosse Close.
1648		Gardners Close
1684	William Colledge	Churchyard Close

APPENDIX II
PLACE NAMES IN THE BRINKLOW ENCLOSURE AWARD of 1742

Barr Lane	In 1742 this was about to be created
The Butts	Land once used for archery practice
Butt Furlong	A furlong was literally the length of a furrow
Wood Furlong	Off Wood Hill
Farther Hungril	In 1742 belonged to James Hancock. Land known to be "hungry" or needing much fertilising to be productive
Hither Hungril	As above but nearer to the village
Rye Furlong	Crop name
Priests Meadow	Glebe land: used to pay the priest's stipend
Priests Bridge	
Priests Lane	In former times the priest would walk to the church along a private secluded lane.
Wood Furlong	
Pedlar's Leys	Leys implies land put down to grass, clover, for a single season or so in contrast to permanent pasture.
Town Furlong	Town suggests the original site of settlement
Lamas Close	Places where grazing was allowed after harvest. Lammas was 1st of August
Lamas Leys	Maybe a clearing where Lammas bread was handed out
Crooked Bush	Probably a landmark

Mill Acres	Probably a water mill
Cures Meadow	Tempting to think "cursed" rather than herbal crops.
Ell Meadow	
Upper Ell and Lower Ell	Ell as in Hill was the third medieval field
Trinity Ell	Owned by Trinity College Cambridge
Ell Lane	Hill Lane. Nothing to do with eels, ells or the sun. Sadly.
Beaumore Field	Interesting because it means "beautiful hill" in Norman French
Over Fosse Furlong	The other sides of the Fosse Way
Cart Arse	Cart House - outbuildings
Newcombs	A comb or coombe was a short valley
Stoney Stitches	Stitch meant a small piece of land
Stitch Gutter	A ditch
King's Piece	Belonging to someone named King. (Richard Kynge in 1332, Monk's Kirby - King's Close)
Hawkers Leys	Land once used for flying hawks
Nunoon	No evidence of nunnery locally, though Bretford had hospice.
The Road called Cow Lane	Track where cows walked to and from for milking etc.
Tutbury Way	An ancient green pathway
Bretford Leys	
Fowler's Furlong	Personal name or where poultry kept.
Stiley Hedge Furlong	Furlong with a hedge and stile.
Furlong against the Hill	The strips along Ell Lane or Wood Hill

Monk Riding Farm Grounds	
Ballands	Infertile land – bad land
Hancock's Leys	
Rooks Nest	A large rookery nearby. Rooks were used as food
Sand and gravel pits lying upon Wood Field	
The Groves	A small wood or group of trees
Arnolds Grove	
Armley	Later Warmly. Probably a personal name
Ley Piece	
Rowneys Piece	
Great Heath	Waste land
Leg Piece	A long narrow field
Gibberds Croft	Pasture usually attached to a dwelling
Ell over Lycence	Footpath over Lycence
Stoopers Lane	A stope is a mark stone, often erected on an old path for pedlars, packmen and other travellers.
Dick and Jacks Grove	
Mutton Hole	Part of the Waste
Ell	Hill
License	Land originally given under licence.
Wood field	Behind Wood Hill, Coombefields

APPENDIX III
BRINKLOW FIELD NAMES FROM THE 1835 GLEBE TERRIER MAP OF THE PARISH

Hill Close	Field, left hand side of Ell Lane bounded by Easenhall Rd.
Dovehouse Close	Next to Ell Close fronting Lutterworth Road. The name may echo a former dove cote, perhaps medieval, even Roman.
Brook Meadows	Several fields bounded by Smite Brook and Ansty Lane
Upper Licence	Right hand side of the Tump behind Ell Lane
Nether Licence	Lower part of field above. Royal licences were needed before fortifications such as Brinklow could be built.
Calves Close	Up to Rugby Rd/All Oaks Lane, Pasture for young cattle. All three fields belonged to William Bailey
College Grounds.	Lutterworth Rd to Smite Brook from canal crossing place. Grounds means area of grassland lying some distance from amin fields. Belonged to the Colledge family.
Clover Close	Crop name, clover being an important fodder crop.
Lamas Close	Lammas land, grazing from 1st August until sowing – Loafmas – a pagan festival = harvest festival.

Three Corner Close	Descriptive. It was and is behind Brook Meadow
Town Furlongs	Behind the original "town" of Brinklow (i.e. The Crescent). A furlong was made up of several strips running in the same direction; it took many top make up an open field.
Sun Furlongs	Possibly a fertile or even very dry area without shade
Rye Furlongs	Adjacent to Brook Meadows. Crop name. Rye was a staple crop.
Far Waterfall	A wet or boggy spot. May be a corruption of Watergall found elsewhere in Warwickshire, implying "nuisance".
Near Waterfall	As above
Such Meadow	Next to above = marshy pasture
Pedlar's Meadow	Footpath used by pedlars and other tavellers,
Pedlar's Leys	As above
Turtis Meadow	A person?
Priest's Meadow	Glebe Land. Tithes on this went to the Rector
Knibbs Close	A personal name or possibly from Knepp, meaning hillock
Long close	Defined by the shape
Long meadow	As above
Croft's Close	A personal name
Old Dairy Ground	Refers to former use, or grazing for a dairy herd
Park Corner Meadow	May refer to ancient land enclosed to keep beasts for hunting
Great Hazel Furlong	A landmark Hazel tree.

Bull Furlong	Where the parish bull was kept when the land was fallow.
Corner Meadow	Self- explanatory
Balance	From Badlands – ie: difficult to work
Little Balance	As above
Great Balance	As above
Yew Tree Hill	Clearly where yew trees grew
Potter's Close	Personal name or more probably site of pottery or brickworks
Stile Hedge Closes	Hedged footpaths with stile between fields
Stile Hedge Meadow	As above
Stripes	From strips recalling the old way of agriculture
Monk's Riding	Coombe lands leased to Brinklow. Not where monks rode!
Monk's Riding Closes	Fields of above
Warmly Close	Probably a personal name – Armley in Enclosure award
Western Gove	Lightly wooded land
Middle Grove	As above
Eastern Grove	As above
Ward's Close	Personal name, or maybe belonging to or leased to a parish officer
Brick Kiln Closes	Site of early quarry and/or brickworks. Good clay deposits there
Brick Kiln Meadows	As above
Sheep Pen Closes	Where sheep were penned for lambing or shearing

King's Closes	Probably a personal name
Hawkers Leys	Early site name - where hawks flown and trained
Twelve Acres	Self -explanatory
Six Acre Closes	As above
Great Bowman's Meadow	Possibly the Butts referred to in the Enclosure award
Little Bowman's Meadow	As above
Fowlers Furlong	Probably a personal name, or where poultry was kept
None Noons	Obscure: just possibly owned by a convent, though none near
High Furzes	scrubland
Little Heath	heathland
Bray's Close	Belonging to the Bray Family
Home Close	Refers to a fields nearest the farmhouse. Brierley's farm now
Stoney Close	Refers to soil type, possibly gravelly
Bingham's Close	Personal name
Fosse Closse	A ditch or maybe the old route of the Fosse Way
Fosse Furlong	As above
Pease Hills	Crop name. Peas widely frown for animal and humans
Great Cart- House	Cart shed. Might refer to Roger Carter or Carecarius of Coombe
Little Cart-House	As above
Collage Closes	Belonging to the Colledge Family
In Hedge Gap	From *ineche* – medieval term for ancient enclosure – land removed from crop rotation of fields
Rail-Pit Close	Can't be anything to do with

	railway. May come from Scandinavian *wray* meaning nook.
Rooks Nest	Rookery and tall trees nearby
Green Lane Close	Recalling the "old green lanes" or ancient trackway (Tutbury Way
Green Lane Meadow	As above
Constable's Close	Land held by the parish Constable
Wood Close	By Burchley Wood
Upper Wood Hills	As above
Lower Wood hills	As Above
Near the Hill	Probably Wood Hill
Woodhall	Corruption of Wood Hill
Heath Closes	Close by the Heathland
Under the Heath	As Above
Wilkin's Heath	Personal name for a waste piece of land
Great Close	Self-explanatory
Little Close	As above
Home Close	As above
Brandon Close	Personal name or a track towards Brandon
Phillip's Close	Personal name
Mutton Hole	Possibly a hollow where sheep collected
Burchley Closes	Burchley fields
North Burchley	As above
Burchley Meadow	As above
Burchley Gap	As above
House Grounds	As above
Below Barn Close	Field with a barn in it
Coppice Corner	Land where woodland was managed by coppicing, or where it had gone out of arable use and left

	to shirt term trees.
Coppice Close	As above

APPENDIX IV
1st JULY 1262 and 28th Aug 1272: "ALL THE FREE MEN, TENANTS OF THE TOWN AND COMMUNITY OF BRINKELAWE"

Name	Likely eventual surname
John the Chaplain	Chaplin
Henry, s/o William,	Williams, Williamson
Adam s/o Roger	Rogers, Rogerson
Henry the Clerk, his brother	Clerk, Clark, Clarke
Gilbert de Wauere	Over
Jordan s/o Thomas	Thomas, Thoms, Thomson
Adam s/o Jordon	Jordan
William Edward	
William de Ardena	Arden
Robert Smith(Faber)	
Hugh Colemon	Coleman
Roger Carter (Caretarius)	
Hugh le King	King
Henry s/o Robert	Roberts, Robertson
Thomas Edward	
William de Mertona	Merton, Marton?
Roger s/o William	
Jordan Marmiun	
Thomas de la Barre	Barr, Barrs
Richard s/o Walter	Walters
Ralph Burges	Burgess
Hugh Pedifer	Pettifer
Henry at the Mill	Miller

28 Aug 1272…..the free men of Brinkelowe, namely:

John the Chaplain	
Gilbert de Wauere	
Hughs/oHenry Sachel	Satchwell
Adam s/oJordan	
John Sutor'	Suter
William Eardward	Edward
Henry atte Chirchende	NB may denote where he lived
William Burges	
William King	
Edward Burges	
William Paris	
John de Hesehull	Hazel
Richard Panci	
Jordan de Ardern	
John s/o Ralph	

Robert de Wolver	
Richard Carter (carectarius)	
Henry Sachel	
Richard de Fosse	
Robert Smith(Faber	
John s/o?	
Hugh Colemon	
Richard King	
Jordan de Ardern lejouene	NB … "the younger"
Ralph s/o Jordan	
John Norman	
Robert de Sireford	
Adam s/o Felicia	
Roger Carter	

John Bering	
Hugh King	
John s/o Hereburg	
Robert Partrich	Partridge
William s/o Henry Townsend (ad finum Ville)	Lived at the end of the village
William de Lalleford	
Thomas Edward	
Roger le Mercer	Mercer
John Auncel	Ansell
Alic' s/o John le Carpenter	
William de Merton	
John s/o Wiliam Cook	
Roger s/o William	
William s/o Ruffe	Rolf, Rufus
William s/o Adam	Adams
Jordan Marmiun	
Mathew s/o Jordan	
Adam Blench	
Henry le Clerke	
William s/o Robert Smith	
William s/o Henry	Harris, Harrison
Jordan s/o Auice	
Richard Coche	Hogg?
Hugh Newcomen	Newcomb
Philip Burges	
Richard Attebare	
Ralph Burges	
William Pedifer	
Robert Attemule	
John s/o Henry Attemule	
William le Faukon	Falcon
Jordan s/o Robert de Fevere	

APPENDIX V
HOUSEHOLD NAMES IN AN 1801 CENSUS FOR BRINKLOW

?	Edward	Croft	John
Adler	David	Cryer	Katherine
Astill	John	Curtis	Thomas
Basely	William	Dalton	Edward
Bason	John?	Dickson	John
Bates	Thomas	Elkington	William
Bayley	George	England	Esther
Bench	James	Everton	Sam
Bird	John	Flude	Mary
Blakemore	John	Goddard	Joseph
Bolton	Thomas	Goode	John
Botterel	Henry	Goodman	William
Bray	Thomas	Green	John
Bray	Mary	Green	James
Bray	Michael	Hayes	Thomas
Brown	JLP?	Hayes	Thomas
Butlin	Wm.	Hayes	John
Checkland	William	Hayes	Sam
Checkland	John	Hayes	Joseph
Checkland	Thomas	Heath	Elizabeth
Clements	Richard	Hewitt	John
Colledge	John	Hiorns	Robert
Colledge	Joseph	Hiorns	Hannah
Colledge	Sarah	Hobley	Edward
Colledge	William	Hobley	Francis
Cooper	E?	Hodgeson	John
Cooper	James	Howe	John

Iliff	Richard	Riley	Thomas
Jackson	Richard	Rogers	Joseph
Jackson	John	Scott	Jos.
Johnson	Michael	Smith	Martha
Johnson	Richard	Smith	John
Jones	Rachel	Sodin	Thomas
Jones	John	Spencer	Thomas
Jones	John	Stean	Mary
Lambley	William	Treen	William
Leader	William	Wale	Edward
Lester	Mary	Walker	William
Lister	John	Walton	John
Malin	John	Watson	J?
Marston	John	Watson	Edward
Mason	Thomas	Webb	Francis
Mason (late)		Webb	Thomas
Matthews	John	Wilkinson	John
Matthews	George	Wilson	Richard
Middleton	Mary	Wolf	Soloman
Mills	Richard	Woodfield	John
More	JLP?	Wright	John
Morris	Charles	Wright	Benjamin
Morson	John		
Morton	Elizabeth		
Owen	Thomas		
Owen	William		
Owen	John		
Owen	Joseph		
Owen (late)			
Parish	Thomas		
Parker	William		
Perry	Ann		
Randel	John		

OUT THERE

Out there, the tumbling children tilt the sky,
Daub the grass green with graffiti laughter,
Deaf to juggernaut time, rumbling after,
Cock snooks as age totters grumbling by.
Up where the jinking church tips its feet high,
Flies the tomb past in cartwheeling rapture;
Blind, to winking childhood's swathing pasture,
The envious dead tell the schoolyard's lie.
In wastage and tillage, the years advance
Roughshod, cavort, on the centuries' way
Through the green village, along the broad road,
While the ancients frown and the children dance.
Out there, in dumb surprise, young heads turn grey,
Pillage the past, to ease the present's load.

Diane Lindsay

Circa 1925. Most names unkown but 2nd row from back, 3rd from right in white top Margaret Boneham nee Peet.. b. 1920

ORIGINAL MEMBERS OF BRINKLOW HISTORY GROUP

Please note this group is no longer in existence and sadly some members are now deceased. The present work is updated entirely through my own researches.

1995   Diane Lindsay (Chairman
1996   Margaret Kent (Treasurer)

Pam Breen
Peter Cross
Kath Cross
Iris Cygan
Margaret Denyer
Len Elliott
Betty Mawson
Dorothy Morgan
Pam Steggles

Long distance members
Douglas Cooke
(Canada)
Pat Cooke (nee
Colledge) (Canada)
Marjorie Simmons
(Canada)

Honorary Members
Peter Kent
George Lindsay

SOURCES: There are almost too many sources to mention by name, but below are some of those which I have found most useful:

Primary:
Census Returns 1841 - 1891
Parish Registers 1558-
The National Archives
Warwick Record Office
Records of Warwick Quarter Sessions
School Log Books 1871-4
Enclosure Award, 1747, Brinklow
Glebe Terrier and Map 1835
Terrier and Map, Oxford Canal 1828
Mrs. Friswell's Diary
Rugby Advertiser back copies on Microfilm.
The British Newspaper Archive
Directories, various
Miss Cryer's Notes
The People of Brinklow

Secondary:
Domesday Book, Warwickshire: transcript and translation Pub Philimore 1976
Victoria County History - Warwick O.U.P 1951
The Antiquities of Warwickshire, Sir William Dugdale (reprint 1891)
The Making of the English Village, W.G. Hoskins(ed.Taylor)Hodder & Stoughton 1988
Tracing Your Ancestors in Warwickshire, F.C. Markwell pub. Birmingham and Midland Society for Genealogy and Heraldry (reprint 1989)

I am also indebted to Brinklow's Story by D. E. Williams, issued in 1967 in conjunction with an Exhibition of Village History in Brinklow, for leading the way, and for inspiring me to want to know even more.

Author's Note to the First Edition

I am not a native of Brinklow. For years, until I started to investigate my family's history, I thought myself the complete "Coventry Kid", being born within the old city walls, going to school and university, marrying, working, and bringing up my children there. To a child growing up in the aftermath of war, whose playgrounds were the bombed buildings clothed with fireweed and the city streets unrelieved by green, Brinklow was "the country", a place you rode to on your bike, looked at with a kind of wistfulness, drank a bottle of lemonade, and rode away from again. Later, Brinklow was its country pubs, a fine place to do a spot of gentle courting in the light summer nights, a quaint village to drive out to and admire on Sunday afternoons. Only when I moved here in 1985, did I come to realise that far from a quiet backwater, this was a living breathing place, with its own pulsating soul, where all of life's human joys and dramas, tears and laughter, pride and little irritations made it so much more than just "that picturesque village on the Fosse Way.

I could never have known, then, that I too would become "quaint", and my home an object of wonder to "tourists", a clue in countless Treasure Hunts. I couldn't have imagined the ease with which I slipped into village life, or the warmth held out from those whose roots went back in Brinklow so much further than mine. I would never have believed how much the village and its history wheedled itself under my skin and into my heart. And, I could never, in a million years, have guessed that my own search for roots would take me back to 1572, to a chap who once bought half of Harborough Magna for £7,and that scores of my ancestors walked these ways before me, and must have known the things my research and my imagination still longs to know. From that time on, I stopped being an "incomer", and felt as if I'd come home.

Diane Lindsay
Brinklow Pottery
10th February 1995

Acknowledgements:

It would be nearly impossible to list and thank all of those people who have helped facilitate the writing of the original *Brynca's Low* and the revision of this second, much larger edition but I will do my best.

Warwick Record Office for permission to reproduce the Glebe Map of 1837, the map of the Brinklow arm of the Oxford Canal and various posters and photographs elsewhere in the book.

The Shakespeare Birthplace Archive for help and enthusiasm with manorial documents

The late **Margaret Kent**, co-founder of the Group, my friend and history companion, sadly taken from us far too soon, whose detective work, transcriptions and utter dedication has been with me throughout.

The late **Mr J.V. Reeves,** for the drawing of Brinklow Castle as it might have been.

Sarah Brice, for alerting to us in the beginning to so many sources for photographs of old Brinklow

Brinklow People, past and present, for advice, for lending and donating photographs, and for sharing memories.

Tony Rattigan for his invaluable help and technical expertise in producing this updated version.

Last but never least, **George Lindsay**, my husband, whose patience, encouragement and photographic expertise has been sterling, and without whom this book and the History Exhibitions would never have come to pass.

Sadly many of the original members of the former Brinklow History Group and those villagers who contributed so much by way of stories, photos and inspiration are no longer with us. I remember them with deep affection.

All errors and omissions are my own, and where possible interested readers should consult the original sources. Every effort has been made to ensure that the information and illustrations herein do not infringe any copyright. The vast majority of images have been sourced from purchased and donated photographs and postcards, some of which have been repaired and renovated to facilitate publication.

Index

Barr Lane, 121, 124, 127

Beatles 1965 film Help, 118

Beeching, 60

Benjamin Tomlinson, 82

Bill Smith, 37, 65, 90

Birchley Wood, 49

Birkley's Coppice, 49

Birmingham Archaeological Society, 40

Black Death, 20

Board of Guardians, 83

Boatees, 55

Bomelau, 13

Brandon Railway bridge, 67

Brandon Silk Throwing Mills, 67

Bray's Close, 121, 133

Bretford, 2, 67, 128

Brick Kiln, 120, 132

Brierley's Farm, 121

Brinchelau, 11

Brinchelawa, 11

Brinklow, 38

Brinklow Aqueduct, 53

Brinklow Arm, 54

Brinklow Canal, 52, 55

Brinklow Castle, 8, 11, 12, 148

Brinklow Cemetery, 26

Brinklow Chapel, 29

Brinklow Church, 4, 28, 35

Brinklow Congregational Chapel, 29, 31

Brinklow Field Names, 130

Brinklow Heath, 3

Brinklow Hill, 2, 4, 9, 11, 16

Brinklow History group, 102

Brinklow Post Office, 30, 72

Brinklow Pottery, 55, 72, 77

Post Office, 61, 76, 77, 79, 91, 99

Post Office Yard, 54, 73, 75, 76

Potter's Close, 121, 132

Priest's Bridge, 120

Prior and Convent of Kenilworth, 20

Pumpkin Deli, 99

Puritans, 21, 22

Quakers, 30

Queen Victoria, 27, 76

R. Emerson, 42

Ratae Coritanorum, 5

Reading Pew, 24

Red Cross Society, 39

Reg Cleaver, 51

Rev. George P. Hattrell, 30

Rev. John Sibree, 30

Reverend J.C. Ritson, 25

Reverend Ritson, 25

Reverend William Fairfax, 34

Richard Cure, 23

Richard de Camville, 10

Richard Rouse Bloxham, 25

Richard Sutton, 57

Rita and Graham Giles, 80

River Avon, 3

Roger de Mowbray, 11, 13, 123

Roman, 2, 4, 5, 18, 21, 130

Round the Revel, 27

Royal British Legion, 27, 92

Rugby Advertiser, 31, 40, 54, 93, 144

Rugby Prisoner of War Fund, 39

Rugby School, 25, 109

Ryton-on Dunsmore, 14

S. Capel, 31

Sally Howe, 65

Sam Mace, 42